Baden-Württemberg

Günther Willmann

Baden-Württemberg

Englische Fassung:
Claudia Spinner

SIGLOCH
EDITION

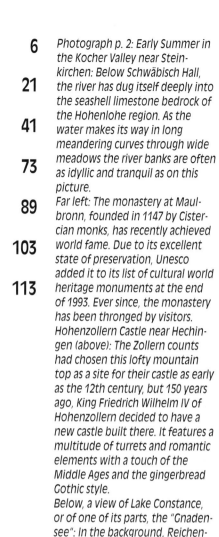

Photograph p. 2: Early Summer in the Kocher Valley near Steinkirchen: Below Schwäbisch Hall, the river has dug itself deeply into the seashell limestone bedrock of the Hohenlohe region. As the water makes its way in long meandering curves through wide meadows the river banks are often as idyllic and tranquil as on this picture.

Far left: The monastery at Maulbronn, founded in 1147 by Cistercian monks, has recently achieved world fame. Due to its excellent state of preservation, Unesco added it to its list of cultural world heritage monuments at the end of 1993. Ever since, the monastery has been thronged by visitors. Hohenzollern Castle near Hechingen (above): The Zollern counts had chosen this lofty mountain top as a site for their castle as early as the 12th century, but 150 years ago, King Friedrich Wilhelm IV of Hohenzollern decided to have a new castle built there. It features a multitude of turrets and romantic elements with a touch of the Middle Ages and the gingerbread Gothic style.

Below, a view of Lake Constance, or of one of its parts, the "Gnadensee": In the background, Reichenau island, and beyond, the "Seerücken" on the Swiss shore, rising 300 meters above lake level.

Bild S. 2: Frühsommer im Kochertal bei Steinkirchen: Unterhalb Schwäbisch Hall hat sich der Fluß tief in die Muschelkalkfelsen des Hohenloher Landes eingefressen. Flußschleifen ziehen durch breite Wiesen, meist geht es an den Ufern auch so idyllisch-ruhig wie hier zu.

Links: Kloster Maulbronn, 1147 von Zisterziensermönchen gegründet, erlangte in jüngster Zeit Weltruhm. Die Gesamtanlage bewog dank ihrer Geschlossenheit die Unesco Ende 1993, Maulbronn in die Liste des Weltkulturerbes aufzunehmen. Seither ist das Kloster ein Besuchermagnet.

Burg Hohenzollern bei Hechingen (oben): Auf dem frei aufragenden Bergkegel stand schon im 12. Jahrhundert die Burg der Zollerngrafen. Hohenzollernkönig Friedrich Wilhelm IV. ließ dort vor 150 Jahren eine neue Burg bauen: vieltürmig, romantisch, mit einem bißchen Mittelalter, mit Gotik und „Zuckerbäckerei".

Rechts ein Eindruck vom Bodensee, genauer von einem seiner Teile, dem Gnadensee: Über Allensbach hinweg geht der Blick zur Insel Reichenau und zum Seerücken, der vom Schweizer Ufer rund 300 Meter ansteigt.

Baden-Württemberg und Stuttgart

Das ist ein Land! Mit Wald, Wein und Wasser, mit hohen Bergen und tiefen Schluchten, Hügeln und Tälern, Kirchen und Klöstern, Burgen und Schlössern und weltweit bekannten Reisezielen von Heidelberg bis zum Bodensee.

Die Bewohner sind „schaffige Leut", darunter Tüftler und Erfinder, die Unternehmen gegründet haben, von denen viele zu internationaler Bedeutung gelangten. Stolz und selbstbewußt bezeichnen die Menschen zwischen Rhein, Neckar, Tauber, Donau und Bodensee ihre Heimat deswegen als „Musterländle". Dieses Ländle mit immerhin um die zehn Millionen Einwohner entstand 1952 durch den nicht ganz frei-willigen Zusammenschluß der alten Länder Baden und Württemberg. Noch heute hegen die Badener so man-che Aversion gegenüber den Schwaben, vor allem, weil deren Metropole Stuttgart zur Hauptstadt des neu-gegründeten Bundeslandes erhoben wurde. Dabei hatte sich gerade hier schon 1120 ein Zusammenschluß vollzogen: Der Markgraf von Baden als Besitzer eines Stutengartens, aus dem dann Stuttgart wurde, ver-heiratete seine Tochter mit einem württembergischen Grafen. Auf dem Gelände des Stutengartens entstand ein Schloß, von dem aus die Württemberger ihr Land lange Zeit regierten.

Stuttgart, die große, kleine Stadt, ob ihrer land-schaftlichen Lage gerühmt, ist umsäumt von Wäldern und Weinbergen, weshalb sie zu Recht mit dem Slogan „Großstadt zwischen Wald und Reben" beschrieben wird. Die Umgebung der schwäbischen Kapitale gibt sich ebenso ländlich wie industriell, es entstand eine Allianz zwischen Acker und Fabrik. So zwängen sich Werkhallen und Gewerbeansiedlungen, Bürohäuser, Schienenstränge, Autobahnen und Hafenbecken zwi-schen die Weinberge und Wälder, zwischen die Obst-wiesen und Felder. Das beeinträchtigte zwar die Lieb-lichkeit der Landschaft, führte aber auch zu einem gesunden Wohlstand. Die Stadt selbst platzt aus allen Nähten, liegt sie doch eingeengt in einem Talkessel, der ihr natürliche Grenzen setzt und zugleich die ihr eigene, südländisch anmutende Schönheit verleiht.

Baden–Württemberg and Stuttgart

What a state! Forests, wines and waters, high mountains and deep gorges, hills and valleys, churches and monasteries, castles and palaces and world-famous points of interest such as Heidelberg and Lake Constance.

Its inhabitants are "industrious people", tinkers and inventors among them, entrepreneurs whose companies gained international importance. Proud and self–confident, the people living between Rhine, Neckar, Tauber, Danube and Lake Constance therefore refer to their region as the „model state". This state with its roughly ten million inhabitants was founded only in 1952, a result of a not completely voluntary merger of the old states Baden and Württemberg. Even today, the inhabitants of Baden harbor some deep-rooted aversions towards the Swabians, especially since the latter´s metropolis Stuttgart was to be the capital of the new state. Yet, it was at this very place where the merger had been foreshadowed as early as 1120, when the margrave of Baden, owner of the „Stutengarten" – later Stuttgart –, gave his daughter in marriage to one of the Württemberg counts. Thus, the „Stutengarten" became the site of a palace which after-wards served as the seat of the House of Württemberg for a long time.

Stuttgart, the big small town, famous for its fabu-lous setting, is surrounded by forests and vineyards, well-deserving of the epithet „city among woods and vines". The region around the Swabian capital is both rural and industrial, fields and factories existing side by side: factory halls and business districts, office buil-dings, railroad tracks, motorways and wet docks bet-ween patches of vinyards and forests, meadows with fruit trees or fields. If this detracts a little from the prettiness of the landscape, it has certainly led to growing prosperity. The city itself is on the verge of bursting it seams, nestled into a valley as it is – a valley that both defines its natural borders and endows it with an own, almost Southern European beauty.

Mark Twain schilderte 1878 eine Floßfahrt auf dem Neckar. Heute verkehren auf dem Fluß Ausflugs- und Frachtschiffe. Im Bild links blicken wir von den Hessigheimer Felsengärten auf Rebhänge und Felder zwischen Besigheim und Mundelsheim. An den Ufern unter den Weinbergen läßt sich's auch herrlich radfahren oder spazieren-gehen.

Originelle, tiefsinnig-humorvolle Lebensart liebt man im deutschen Südwesten. Auch Dramatisches: Der Schwabe Friedrich Schiller (rechts auf dem Stuttgarter Schillerplatz) wird als deutscher Klassiker hoch verehrt. Geschätzt ist aber auch der Küfermeister, der die Fässer für den Wein herstellt.

In 1878, Mark Twain described a rafting trip down the Neckar. Today, the river accommodates both freight and leisure boats. The picture on the left side shows a view from the Hessigheim rock gardens onto the vineyards and fields between Besigheim and Mundelsheim. The river banks on the foot of the vineyards are ideal for bicycle tours or walks.

The people in Southwestern Germany display a thoughtful, humorous attitude towards life. They are also fond of the dramatic: Friedrich Schiller (above at Schillerplatz square in Stuttgart), a native of Swabia, is a highly revered dramatist of German classicism. The master cooper who fashions wine casks is also held in high esteem, however.

Thaddäus Troll, der den Bestseller „Deutschland, Deine Schwaben" schrieb, sah in seiner Heimatstadt Stuttgart „Hügelketten, die sich dem Häusermeer entgegenstemmen", für ihn war die Stadt ein „brodelnder Kessel, der überläuft", und es schmeckte hier „nach Laugenbrezeln, Maschinenöl und Auspuffgas, nach herbem Trollinger und warmem Leberkäs". Die Lage im Talkessel des Nesenbachs, eines verdolten Zuflusses des Neckar, hat ihre besonderen Reize, die von vielen Dichtern besungen wurden. Am rechten Rand des Bildes ist gerade noch der denkmalgeschützte Hauptbahnhof zu sehen, der Mittelpunkt der künftigen City „Stuttgart 21" werden soll. Der Turm mit dem Stern gilt als eines der Wahrzeichen der Stadt. Einen viel älteren zeigt die Mitte, den vom Alten Schloß, daneben Schloßplatz mit Neuem Schloß, Königsbau und Schillerplatz. Und ganz links ragt der Tagblatt-Turm empor, 1928 eingeweiht, ein Architekturbeispiel seiner Zeit.

Thaddäus Troll, author of the best-seller "Germany, Your Swabians", saw his hometown surrounded by "ranges of hills pressing against a sea of houses", for him the city was "a bubbling cauldron on the brink of boiling over", smelling of "pretzels, machine oil and exhaust fumes, dry Trollinger wine and warm bologna". Its site in the hollow of the valley of the Nesenbach, a Neckar affluent which has been covered and incorporated into the city canal system, endows the city with a special charm praised by quite a number of poets. At the right margin of the picture, the Central Railway Station, a protected monument intended to become the hub of the new "Stuttgart 21" city concept. The tower with the star is a landmark of the city. Others, much older, may be found in the center: the Old Palace next to Schloßplatz square and the New Palace, Königsbau and Schillerplatz square. Finally, to the very left, the "Tagblatt"-Tower, finished in 1928, a prime example of the architecture of the time.

Die sich weit ausdehnenden Grün-
anlagen im Zentrum haben ihren
eigentlichen Ursprung im einstigen
Stutengarten, der sich zum fürstlichen Park entwickelte. Gleich
zwei Theater stehen dort: das
Große und das Kleine Haus – für
Oper, Ballett und Schauspiel. In der
Oper – im Hintergrund zu sehen –
sang schon Caruso, inszenierte
Wieland Wagner und choreo-
graphierte John Cranko, der das
Stuttgarter Ballett zu Weltruhm
führte. Im unzerstört gebliebenen
Großen Haus wurde aber auch
weltbewegende Politik gemacht:
Am 6. September 1946 hielt der
amerikanische Außenminister
James F. Byrnes die Rede, die
Deutschland wieder den Weg zu
einer freien, selbständigen Nation
ebnete.

The extensive park at the center
of the city originated in the so-
called Stutengarten, which later
was incorporated into the palace
gardens. Two theaters are to be
found there: the "Großes Haus"
and the "Kleines Haus" for opera,
ballet and theater performances.
Visitors to the opera house – in
the background – have heard
Caruso sing, seen Wieland
Wagner's stage productions and
watched John Crankos´s choreo-
graphy, which led the Stuttgart
ballet company to world fame.
The "Großes Haus", spared in the
war, also was the site of world
politics: There, on September 6,
1946, the American Secretary of
State James F. Byrnes made the
speech which was to smooth the
way for Germany to once more
become a free, independent
nation.

Stuttgarts pulsierendes Herz:
Neues Schloß und Schloßplatz
(links) und Stiftskirche mit Schillerplatz und Fruchtkasten (rechts).
Herzog Carl Eugen von Württemberg, ein nach Macht strebender
Fürst in Europa, war 18, als er 1746
mit dem Bau seines Residenz-
schlosses begann. 1944 wurde das
neue Schloß zerstört, nach dem
Wiederaufbau fanden zwei Mini-
sterien und die Repräsentations-
räume der Landesregierung hier
einen guten Platz. Besonders
hervorzuheben ist dabei der
restaurierte Marmorsaal.
Im Bild rechts beeindrucken die
zwei charakteristischen Türme der
traditionsreichen Stiftskirche. Die
evangelische Hauptkirche geht auf
ein mittelromanisches Kirchlein
zurück, das 1240 zu einer drei-
schiffigen, spätromanischen
Basilika erweitert wurde. Der
Fruchtkasten, in der Gotik errich-
tet, in der Renaissance umgebaut,
beherbergt heute die Musikinstru-
mentensammlung des Landes-
museums.

Stuttgart's pulse: New Palace and
Schloßplatz square (left), and the
Stiftskirche church with Schillerplatz square and Fruchtkasten
(right). Duke Carl Eugen of Württemberg, striving for power within
Europe, was 18 years old when
he had the foundations to his
residential palace laid in 1746. The
New Palace was destroyed in 1944,
and today, after its restoration,
houses two ministries as well as
representational rooms of the
state government. The splendor
of the restored marble room is
remarkable.
The picture on the left shows the
two characteristic steeples of the
historic Stiftskirche. This major
protestant church dates back to a
small church from the middle
Romanesque period, extended in
1240 into a three-aisled basilica in
the late Romanesque style. The
so-called Fruchtkasten, a Gothic
building remodeled in the
Renaissance, today is the domicile
of the state museum´s collection
of musical instruments.

Die Neue Staatsgalerie ist ein Bau des englischen Architekten James Stirling, der viele Besucher nach Stuttgart lockt. Farbintensiv aus Glas, Naturstein und Metall geschaffen, stellt das Gebäude im Äußeren wie im Inneren ein Meisterwerk dar. König Wilhelm I. ließ 1838 bis 1842 ein Museum der bildenden Künste errichten, aus dem dann die Staatsgalerie mit Alt- und Neubau hervorging. Hier wird Malerei vom Mittelalter bis zum 19. Jahrhundert gezeigt, mit Hauptwerken aller wichtigen Epochen, Schulen und Nationen. Hinzu kommen eine umfassende grafische Sammlung und der wohl bedeutendste Bestand an europäischen Handzeichnungen und Druckgrafiken aus dem 20. Jahrhundert. Im Stirlingbau herrscht die klassische Moderne vor: Picasso, Beckmann, Chagall, Braque, Kokoschka, Dix, Klee, Baumeister, Schlemmer und viele andere mehr.

The New State Gallery, a building by the British architect James Stirling, is a prime reason for many people to visit Stuttgart. Richly colored and built of glass, natural stone and metal, the structure is simply a masterpiece, both outside and inside. The predecessor of the State Gallery and its old and new buildings was a museum for the Fine Arts built from 1838 to 1842 under the auspices of King Wilhelm I. Today, the Old Gallery features paintings from the Middle Ages to the 19th century, with major works from all important epochs, traditions and countries. Additionally, there is an extensive display of graphic sheets and perhaps the most significant collection of drawings and prints from the 20th century. The building by Stirling is dedicated to classical modernism: Picasso, Beckmann, Chagall, Braque, Kokoschka, Dix, Klee, Baumeister, Schlemmer, among many others.

Das Daimler-Benz-Museum in Untertürkheim ist ein Juwel der Technik – und der Ästhetik. Es darf als einmalig bezeichnet werden, denn lückenlos werden die Produkte der beiden Automobil-Erfinder von 1885 an gezeigt: wohlgepflegte, teilweise noch fahrbereite Veteranen wie die ersten funktionstüchtigen Motorkutschen von Gottlieb Daimler und Carl Benz. Aber auch traumhaft schöne Modelle aus den 20er und 30er Jahren, dazu Boliden aus fünf Jahrzehnten Renngeschichte sowie Flug- und Schiffsmotoren. Der V10-Motor F01 10E, eines der neuesten Aggregate, interessiert technisch Versierte besonders als heißes Kraftpaket der Formel 1. Oben: der erste Motor mit einer Bosch-Magnetzündung. Auch Robert Bosch gehört zu den berühmten Tüftlern im Schwabenland.

DIE ERSTEN AUTOMOBILE

1886 Benz Patent-Motor

The Daimler-Benz-Museum at Untertürkheim is quite a jewel, both with respect to technolog[y] and aesthetics. The comprehensive show of products by the tw[o] automobile inventors, with piec[es] dating all the way back to 1885, may well be called unique: Some of the well-preserved veterans like the first motor coaches by Gottlieb Daimler and Carl Benz s[till] function today, and gorgeous models from the twenties and thirties, historic racing cars from five decades as well as airplane and ship engines are waiting to [be] admired. The V10 engine F01 10E, one of the newest sets, is especially interesting for technology fans: It's the muscle package of Formula 1 races. Far left: The first engine featuring the Bosch magnetical ignition. Robert Bosc[h], too, was one of the more famou[s] tinkerers from Swabia.

Daß Baden-Württemberg in technischer Hinsicht auf so viele Erfolge stolz sein darf, verwundert nicht. Das Land ohne Bodenschätze war von jeher auf das Sinnieren und Erfinden angewiesen, um den Menschen Arbeit und Brot zu geben. Ohne voneinander zu wissen, entwickelten ein Badener und ein Württemberger die ersten Autos der Welt, Carl Benz in Mannheim das „Motor-Veloziped" auf drei Rädern, Gottlieb Daimler in Cannstatt seine vierrädrige Motorkutsche. Der Markenname Mercedes kam auf, weil ein international erfolgreicher Automobil-Kaufmann für die Produkte einen einprägsamen Namen suchte. Er fand ihn im Vornamen seiner Tochter – Mercedes.

It is hardly surprising that Baden-Württemberg can be proud of so many technical success stories. The people of this state lacking mineral resources have always had to rely on their powers of imagination and invention to earn their livelihood. Without knowing of each other, a native of Baden and an inhabitant of Württemberg simultaneously developed the first cars in the world – Carl Benz his "motor velociped" on three wheels at Mannheim and Gottlieb Daimler his four–wheeled motor coach at Cannstatt. The brandname Mercedes emerged when an internationally successful automobile dealer was looking for a catchy name for the products and found it in the name of his daughter Mercedes.

Stuttgart ist, wie ganz Baden-Württemberg, eine kulinarische Reise wert. Schon Goethe ließ seinen Reineke Fuchs sagen: „Laßt uns nach Schwaben entfliehen, dort gibt es des Guten in Hülle und Fülle." Das ist noch immer so. (Hier gilt der Wahlspruch: „Essen und Trinken hält Leib und Seele zusammen.") Die Reben wachsen bis in die City hinein, Mineralwasser sprudelt aus vielen Quellen. Es gibt innerhalb der Markungsgrenzen noch Bauerndörfer, und einmal im Jahr findet im Stadtzentrum ein gemütliches Fest statt, das „Weindorf". Am Rotenberg (Bild links) gedeiht, neben anderen Sorten, der Lieblingswein vieler Schwaben, der Trollinger.

Like all of Baden–Württemberg, Stuttgart is well worth a trip. Already Goethe had his figure Reinecke Fuchs exclaim: "Let's make our way to Swabia, there is plenty of good stuff to be had!" This still rings true today: According to a local motto "eating and drinking keep together body and soul." Grapes even grow in the city, and mineral water bubbles up from a wealth of sources. The city limits include rural villages, and once a year an easy–going festival takes possession of the center: the "Weindorf". At the Rotenberg (left), the famous Trollinger – favorite wine of many Swabians – thrives among other kinds of grapes.

nnereien sind in der schwäbischen und in der badischen Küche sehr beliebt. Herz, Leber und Nieren, würzig zubereitet, zählen zu den Spezialitäten, genauso wie Kutteln, die in Frankreich Tripes und in Italien Trippa heißen. Im Schwabenland werden sie meist "sauer" gegessen, in Rot- oder Weißwein, mit Brot oder Röstkartoffeln.

Einzigartig auf der Welt sind die Maultaschen, eine geradezu typische Erfindung der schwäbischen Hausmannskost (Bild ganz rechts). Als Fastenspeise gedacht, also fleischlos, wurde in die Teighülle neben Spinat und Kräutern auch Kalbsbrät hineingeschmuggelt, um den lieben Gott zu überlisten.

Gaisburger Marsch (rechts) ein Gericht, das zum ersten Mal im Stuttgarter Stadtteil Gaisburg für Soldaten gekocht wurde: ein Eintopf mit Fleischbrühe, Kartoffeln, Spätzle, Siedfleisch und jedweder Phantasie. Fein geschmelzt mit Butter und Zwiebeln eine Leibspeise für echte Schwaben!

Unten rechts: ein historisches Rezept für Mandelmus und Mandelsuppe. Fast 600 Jahre alt, soll es vom Koch der Burg Wirtemberg stammen, die einstmals auf dem Rotenberg über den Stuttgarter Stadtteilen Untertürkheim und Uhlbach stand.

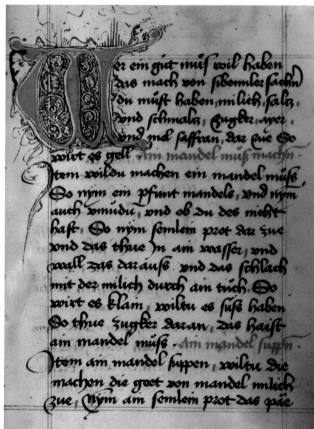

Innards are very popular in the cuisines of Baden and Württemberg. Heart, liver and kidneys, prepared with aromatic seasonings, are a specialty, as is tripe, i.e. French tripes and Italian trippa. In Swabia, tripe is usually eaten "sour", i.e. marinated in red or white wine, and served with bread or roasted potatoes (left above).

Maultaschen, a kind of ravioli, are typical of Swabian country cooking (right above). Originally meant as a Lenten dish, i.e. meatless, ground veal was sometimes smuggled into the filling along with spinach and herbs – trying to outsmart the Lord Above.

Gaisburger Marsch (left below), a dish first prepared for soldiers at the Stuttgart suburb Gaisburg. The stew is made from meat broth, potatoes, Spätzle, boiled meats and anything else in the cook's fancy: Topped with onions browned in butter, it is a favorite with every true native of Swabia!

Right below: A historical recipe for almond purée and almond soup. It is almost 600 years old and said to have originated with the cook of Wirtemberg Castle, which formerly towered on the Rotenberg above the suburbs Untertürkheim and Uhlbach.

Der Schwarzwald

Die Römer nannten ihn „Silva Nigra", schwarzer, dunkler Wald, der für sie unheimlich war, weil er undurchdringlich schien. Doch das ist viele Jahrhunderte her. Längst wurde der *Black Forest* zu einer der beliebtesten Ferienlandschaften in Deutschland. Als ein Naturereignis fasziniert der noch immer urtümlich anmutende Wald Menschen unserer Zeit, die aus dem Beton und Asphalt der Städte kommen. Der Schwarzwald ist ein langes, recht schmales Mittelgebirge: 160 km von Nord nach Süd, an der breitesten Stelle 60 km von West nach Ost. Im Süden ragen hohe Berge auf, Feldberg, Herzogenhorn und Belchen, deren Gipfel Höhen von über 1400 m aufweisen, im nördlichen Teil erreicht die Hornisgrinde 1164 m über dem Meer.

Im Mittelalter zogen Einsiedler in den Tann, Klöster entstanden, Mönche rodeten und kultivierten die Wildnis. Bauern siedelten und betrieben Ackerbau. Dann lernten sie die Bäume des Waldes als Bauholz zu verkaufen, fällten die Stämme und trieben sie als Flöße auf den heimischen Gewässern und dem Rhein bis nach Holland. Die Flotte der Niederländer bestand aus Tannen und Fichten des Schwarzwalds.

Auch die Glasindustrie verbrauchte Unmengen an Holz. Es diente zudem als Brennstoff zum Verhütten von Erz. So war im 17. Jahrhundert der halbe Schwarzwald kahlgeschlagen und „verheizt". An Wiederaufforstung dachte damals noch niemand, viele Gemeinden verarmten so schnell, wie sie aufgeblüht waren. Der Raubbau hatte jedoch auch seine Vorteile, sorgte er doch für einen lichteren Charakter des Schwarzwalds. Die bedrückende Düsternis wich einer aufgelockerten, freundlichen Landschaft. Auch die Menschen wurden fröhlicher, aufgeschlossener. Sie kamen mit der Welt in Verbindung und gingen in die Welt hinaus. Und in ihre hübschen, nach wie vor häufig von hohen Bäumen umgebenen Dörfer und Weiler kamen Fremde, Besucher aus den umliegenden Städten und aus anderen Ländern. Die schätzten den Wald und die in ihm sprudelnden Heilquellen überaus, ebenso aber die so berühmten Weinlagen am Rande des Schwarzwalds. Kein Wunder also, daß sich der Schwarzwald in touristischer Hinsicht Weltgeltung verschafft hat.

The Black Forest

It was called "silva nigra" by the Romans, a black, dark forest inspiring fear since it seemed to be impenetrable. But this was many centuries ago. The Black Forest has long since evolved into one of the most popular holiday regions in Germany. The forest, which still makes a bit of a primeval impression, is a natural wonder and especially fascinating to people living in today´s concrete and asphalt-ridden cities. It consists of a long, rather narrow band of mountains measuring 160 kilometers from north to south and 60 kilometers from west to east at its widest point. The high peaks are in the south – Feldberg, Herzogenhorn and Belchen with an altitude of more than 1400 meters –, whereas in the north, the highest elevation Hornisgrinde comes up to 1164 meters above sea level.

In the Middle Ages, hermits sought solitude among the blackish pines, monasteries were founded, monks cleared and cultivated the wilderness. The area was settled with peasants who tilled the soil. Having realized that trees could be sold for timber, they soon started lumbering, and raftsmen drove floats of trunks down local rivers into the Rhine, and all the way to Holland. The Dutch fleet was made of yew and spruce trees from the Black Forest.

The glass industry, too, needed large quantities of wood, and so did the smelting of ore. In the 17th century, half of the Black Forest was cleared and used up. At that time, reforestation was not an issue, and many communities became poor as quickly as they had got rich. – This destructive lumbering had its benefits too, however. As the forest became less dense, oppressive darkness was replaced by a lighter, friendlier landscape. In turn, the people turned more cheerful and sociable as they came into contact with other people and went out into the world. And their pretty villages and hamlets, more often than not surrounded by high trees, were frequented by strangers, visitors from nearby cities and foreign countries. They came for the forest and its medicinal springs, and, finally, for the famous vineyards in the foothills of the Black Forest. It is no surprise, then, that the Black Forest is popular among tourists from all over the world.

Links ein besonders typisches Schwarzwaldhaus, es ist der Vogtsbauernhof und bildet den Kern des gleichnamigen Freilichtmuseums im Gutachtal nahe Hausach. Alle anderen Baudenkmale, die dort zu sehen sind, wurden an anderen Orten im mittleren und südlichen Schwarzwald abgetragen und hier wieder aufgebaut. Rechts oben sowie unten zwei Schwarzwälderinnen: eine ganz normal mit dem roten Bollenhut, dem weltberühmten Trachtensymbol, das jedoch offiziell nur unverheiratete Frauen aus ganzen drei Gemeinden im Gutachtal tragen. Die andere ganz verrückt als Hexe, als Figur der schwäbisch-alemannischen Fasnacht. Wer aber glaubt, die Hexe sei weiblichen Geschlechts, täuscht sich fast immer: Unter der Maske verbirgt sich in der Regel ein Mann.

Far left, an archetypical Black Forest house, the Vogtsbauernhof, showpiece of the outdoor museum of the same name in the Gutach valley near Hausach. All other buildings to be admired at the museum were dismantled at their original sites in the Black Forest and then faithfully rebuilt here.
Above and to the left, two Black Forest women: one dressed quite ordinarily, with the knobby red hat which has become a symbol for the traditional Black Forest costume world-wide, although originally only unmarried women of all but three communities in the Gutach valley wore it, the other disguised as a witch, a prominent figure of the Swabian-Alemannic Mardi Gras tradition. People who think that such witches are female are almost always wrong, however: Usually, it's a man hiding beneath the mask.

Ein herrliches Bild aus dem Nord-
schwarzwald: die Wiedenfelsen im
oberen Bühlertal, südlich von
Rastatt, ein Bild wie ein Gemälde
von Caspar David Friedrich. Das
13 km lange Bühlertal ist als Land-
schaftsschutzgebiet ausgewiesen,
in dem es sich wunderbar wan-
dern läßt. Von Bühl talaufwärts
geht ein Weg erst noch an Reb-
hängen, dann steilen Obstbaum-
wiesen vorbei, später durch die
Gertelbachschlucht mit Wasserfällen hinauf zu den aus dem Berg-
wald aufragenden Wiedenfelsen.
Wer noch weiter will, „sammelt"
vielleicht einige Tausender ober-
halb der Schwarzwaldhochstraße:
Mehliskopf, Hochkopf, Hornisgrinde. – Nach der Wanderung
schmeckt der örtliche Wein, der
Bühlertaler Riesling oder der
Affentaler Spätburgunder. Hier ge-
deihen aber auch die berühmten
Bühler Zwetschgen, die Anlaß
geben, alljährlich im August ein
fröhliches Zwetschgenfest zu
feiern.

A marvelous picture from the northern part of the Black Forest: the Wiedenfelsen rock in the upper Bühlot valley, south of Rastatt, a picture that could be taken from a painting by Caspar David Friedrich. The Bühlot valley is about 13 kilometers long and a protected area, great for hiking. Starting at Bühl, the main path goes up the valley, initially past vineyards, then along steep meadows with fruit trees, later through the Gertelbach gorge with its waterfalls and all the way up to the Wiedenfelsen rock projecting from the forest. Along the "Schwarzwaldhochstraße" highway, people with a taste for more may add a few mountains of more than thousand meters to their list: Mehliskopf, Hochkopf, Hornisgrinde. After the hike, one might enjoy a bottle of local wine such as Bühlertaler Riesling or Affentaler Spätburgunder. The famous Bühler Zwetschgen plums, too, are grown here and provide the occasion for a lively plum festival in August each year.

*Die Uhren und der Schwarzwald –
ein Synonym. In früheren Zeiten
brachten Uhrenträger – im Bild
oben und ganz oben rechts als
Holzskulpturen – die kunstvoll
gestalteten, heimgefertigten
Erzeugnisse in viele Länder Euro-
pas. Sie waren monatelang unterwegs und wurden von ihren
Stammkunden immer sehnlichst
erwartet. Ganz rechts unten:
Trachtenträger bei einem Heimat-
fest als Uhrenträger.*

*Die größte Kuckucksuhr der Welt
steht in Schonach (rechts). Sie
wurde als Schwarzwaldhäuschen
gestaltet, über 3 m hoch, reich
verziert und mit Blumen über-
laden. Der 80 cm große Kuckuck
zeigt sich, wenn ihn der Uhren-
schlag ruft, in der Dachluke.
Kuckuck!*

Die ersten Schwarzwälder Uhren entstanden im 17. Jahrhundert auf den Höfen um Furtwangen. Sie waren ganz einfach, ganz aus Holz, mit nur einem Zeiger. Im 18. Jahrhundert wurden Schlag- und Musikwerke eingebaut. Allmählich entwickelte sich eine florierende Industrie, aus Bauern wurden Fabrikanten, deren Uhren zu begehrten Artikeln in aller Welt. 1740 stellte Franz Ketterer die erste Uhr mit dem Kuckuck her. Das Klapptürchen im Uhrengiebel, das sich für den lustigen Vogel öffnet, ist allerdings eine Erfindung des 19. Jahrhunderts. Auf hölzernen Gestellen getragen, erreichten die holzgeschnitzten Gehäuse mit den Uhrwerken die Märkte in fernen Ländern.

The first Black Forest clocks were made in the 17th century on farms around Furtwangen. They were quite simple, carved entirely out of wood, with only one hand. In the 18th century, striking mechanisms and musical devices were added. A flourishing industry gradually developed, peasants became manufacturers as their clocks became popular all over the world. In 1740, Franz Ketterer made the first clock that featured a cuckoo. The little hinged door in the clock´s gable-end, which opens for the merry little bird, is a 19th century invention, however. The clockworks and their carved wooden cases were carried to far-away foreign markets on special wooden racks.

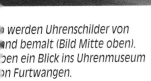

werden Uhrenschilder von
nd bemalt (Bild Mitte oben).
ben ein Blick ins Uhrenmuseum
on Furtwangen.

ne Schwarzwälder Uhr besonde-
r Art (Bild rechts), ein Werk aus
eustadt, geschaffen um 1800. Sie
ommt einem kleinen Kunstwerk
eich, geschmackvoll bemalt,
hlicht im Design und ohne
uckuck. Die Zeit wird durch
ötentöne und sieben Melodien
ngegeben.

The Black Forest and clocks are
almost synonymous. In earlier
times, clock carriers – to the left
and above in the form of wooden
sculptures – took the skilfully
fashioned clocks, which were
usually made at home, to many
European countries. The carriers
were on the road for months at a
time, with customers waiting for
them anxiously. Bottom left: Men
in the traditional costume of a
clock carrier at a regional festival.

The world's largest cuckoo's clock
is to be found at Schonach (left). It
was made to look like a Black
Forest house and is more than
3 meters high, ornately carved and
ladden with flowers. The cuckoo
measures 80 centimeters and
emerges from the attic window
when the clock strikes. Cuckoo!

The faces of the clocks are painted
by hand (above middle).
To the left, the clock museum at
Furtwangen.
A very special Black Forest clock
(right), dating from 1800. Its clock-
work was made at Neustadt. The
clock is a small work of art, taste-
fully painted, its shape unpreten-
tious and without a cuckoo.
The hours are announced by the
sounds of a flute and seven
melodies.

Im Schwarzwald ragen die höchsten Erhebungen des Landes Baden-Württemberg auf. Sie bieten weite Ausblicke. Links sieht man vom Belchen hinab nach Neuenweg und hinüber in die Schweizer Alpen. Mit seiner hohen, freien Kuppe ist der Belchen – 1414 m hoch – zwar nur der dritthöchste, aber für viele der schönste Berg des Schwarzwalds. Über der Baumgrenze macht sich an ihm eine subalpine Flora breit: auf den Felsen wachsen Steingewächse, man findet auch Glockenblumen und den Fingerhut.

Bei Triberg (Bild rechts) stürzt sich die Gutach in sieben Stufen zwischen gewaltigen Granitblöcken 162 m in die Tiefe. Ein Wanderweg führt mindestens eine halbe Stunde lang an den Triberger Wasserfällen empor.
Empfehlenswert ist auch, das Triberger Heimatmuseum aufzusuchen, in dem viel von dem gezeigt wird, was früher zum Alltagsleben gehört hat: Kleider und Trachten, Handwerkszeug und Geräte aus der Landwirtschaft, aber auch Erzeugnisse der Glasindustrie, mundgeblasen, sowie Spieluhren und Orchestrien. Überaus aufschlußreich ist ein Modell der von Konstanz nach Offenburg führenden Schwarzwaldbahn mit ihren 36 Tunnels allein zwischen St. Georgen und Hornberg. Sie entstand 1863 bis 1873 und gilt als Vorbild der weltberühmten Gotthardstrecke in der Schweiz.

The highest altitudes in Baden-Württemberg are to be found in the Black Forest, offering extensive panoramic views. To the left side, a view from the Belchen to Neuenweg and beyond, onto the Swiss Alps. The Belchen – 1414 meters high – with its lofty, bare top only comes in third, but for many people it is the most beautiful mountain in the Black Forest. Above the timber-line, the mountain is covered with subalpine flora: rock plants clinging to the crevices, bluebells and digitalis in abundance.

Near Triberg (left), the Gutach river needs seven steps to plunge down 162 meters between huge boulders of granite. A path provides a magnificent half-an-hour hike alongside the Triberg waterfalls.
The local museum at Triberg is also worth visiting, featuring a multitude of items that used to belong to everyday life: Clothes and costumes, tools and agricultural equipment, mouth-blown products of the glass industry as well as music boxes and orchestria. A prototype of the Black Forest railway line running between Constance and Offenburg, with its 36 tunnels between St. Georgen and Hornberg, is quite an interesting object for study. It was built from 1863 to 1873 and is said to have been the model for the world-famous St. Gotthard railway in Switzerland.

27

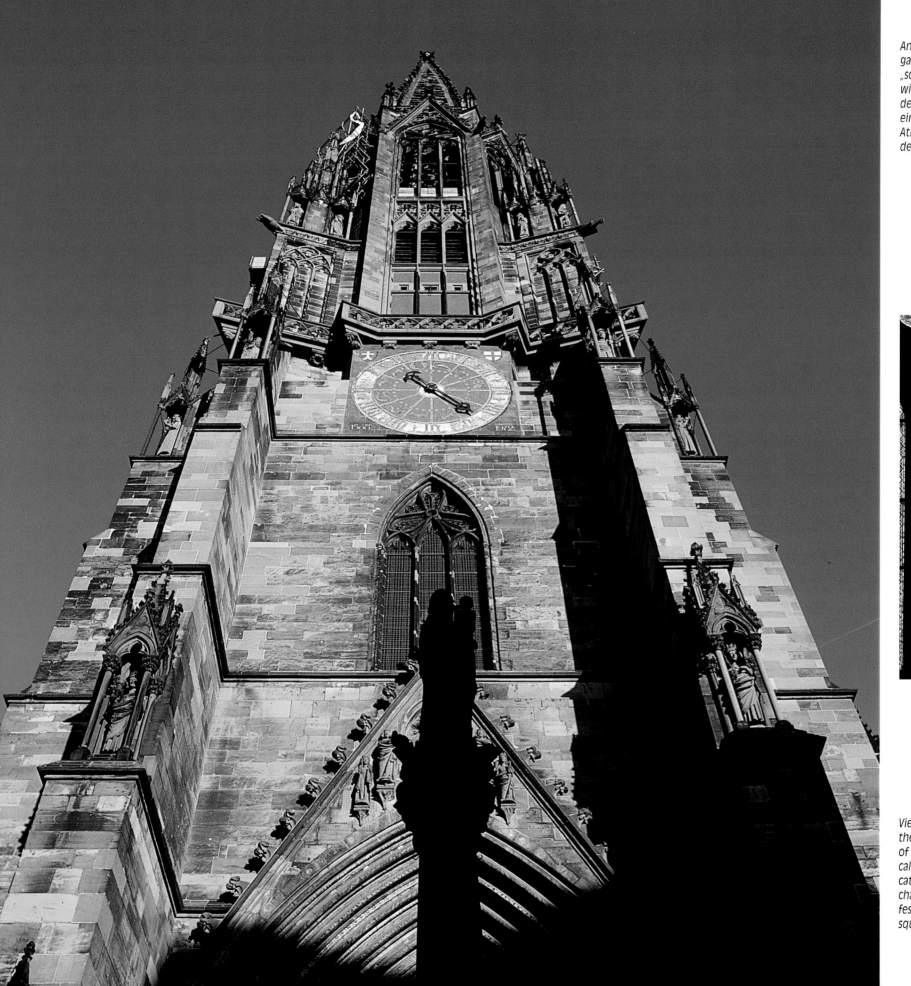

Ansichten von Freiburg im Breisgau: Links erhebt sich der „schönste Turm der Christenheit", wie gerne gesagt wird, der Turm des gotischen Münsters. Unten eines der Chorfenster. Rechts: Atmosphäre beim Straßenfest auf dem Rathausplatz.

Views of Freiburg im Breisgau: To the left, the "most beautiful tower of Christianity", as people like to call it, the spire of the Gothic cathedral. Above, one of the chancel windows. Right: Street festival scene on Rathausplatz square.

Freiburg gilt als die Hauptstadt des Schwarzwaldes. Die alte Universitätsstadt hat aber auch ihre Beziehungen zur Oberrheinebene, zum Kaiserstuhl und über die nahe französische und schweizerische Grenze. Freiburg liegt am Rande der Berge und wendet sich den Talauen des großen Flusses zu. Vom 116 m hohen Turm des Münsters ist dies gut zu erkennen. Der Blick auf die Stadt zeigt den Marktplatz zu Füßen des Münsters, gesäumt von stilecht restaurierten Bürgerhäusern. Wenige Schritte vom Münsterplatz entfernt liegt der kastanienbestandene Rathausplatz mit dem Neuen Rathaus, das einst das Zentrum der 1457 gegründeten Universität war, mit dem Alten Rathaus und der Gerichtslaube aus dem 13. Jahrhundert. Die altertümlichen Gassen und die Bächle, die winzigen Wasserkanäle, von denen Freiburg durchzogen wird, geben der ehrwürdigen Stadt ihr besonderes Gepräge.

Freiburg is looked upon as the capital of the Black Forest. The old university town also has its affiliations with the Upper Rhine Valley, however, with the Kaiserstuhl mountains and the nearby French and Swiss borderlands. Freiburg is situated on the edge of the mountains, facing the lowlands in the big river valley, as may easily be discerned from the tower of the cathedral. A view onto the town shows the market square at the foot of the cathedral, framed by faithfully restored houses of wealthy citizens. Rathausplatz square, planted with chestnuts, is only a few steps away from cathedral square. The new city hall was formerly the center of the university, founded in 1457, and the old city hall and the court loggia date from the 13th century. Old-fashioned alleyways and rivulets, tiny water canals all over the city, give the old town a special character.

Links das wunderschön in die
Landschaft gefügte Kloster
St. Peter, rechts der erhabene
Innenraum der Klosterkirche.
Unten die Rokoko-Bibliothek mit
über 30 000 Bänden und allegori-
schen Figuren auf der Galerie.

On the left, the monastery
St. Peter, beautifully nestled into
the landscape, on the right, an
interior view of the monastery
church. Below, the rococo library
with its more than 30,000 volumes
features allegorical figures on the
gallery.

Im Schwarzwald stehen mehrere, meist von Benediktinern gegründete Klöster.
St. Peter – zwischen Freiburg und Furtwangen gelegen – war eines der wichtigsten.
Berühmt sind auch St. Blasien südlich des Schluchsees, St. Märgen östlich von St. Peter,
St. Ulrich südlich von Freiburg, St. Trudpert im Münstertal und nicht zuletzt Hirsau bei
Calw, heute nur noch Ruine, einst jedoch wegweisend und höchst einflußreich.

The Black Forest is the site of several monasteries, most of which were founded
by the Benedictine order. St. Peter – between Freiburg and Furtwangen – was one of the
most important. St. Blasien south of Schluchsee lake, St. Märgen east of St. Peter, St.
Ulrich south of Freiburg and St. Trudpert in the Münster valley are equally famous, and
so was Hirsau near Calw, today only a ruin, but once exemplary and highly influential.

Narren und Hexen – sie gehören zur Fasnacht in Villingen und Kappelrodeck, in Zell am Harmersbach, in Oberndorf und in vielen anderen Orten im Schwarzwald, an seinen Rändern und auf der angrenzenden Schwäbischen Alb. Das bekannteste Narrennest der Region dürfte Rottweil sein, die schmucke, ehemals freie Reichsstadt am Neckar. Ihr historischer „Narrensprung" zieht Jahr für Jahr Besucher aus nah und fern an. Zu den hölzernen Masken gehören das buntscheckige „Häs", das Gewand, und das Geschell, das fürchterlichen Lärm macht. Die Masken werden von Kunsthandwerkern hergestellt – siehe oben; neben dem Schnitzer betätigt sich der Masken-Maler (ganz rechts).

Fools and witches – they belong to the Mardi Gras activities at Villingen and Kappelrodeck, at Zell am Harmersbach, at Oberndorf and at many other places in the Black Forest, its borderlands and the adjacent Schwäbische Alb mountains. The most famous den of fools in the region may well be Rottweil, the pretty, formerly free city on the Neckar. Every year, its historical "Narrensprung" event draws visitors from near and far. The wooden masks are complimented by colorful "Häs", i.e. garments, and the "Geschell", a contraption which emits ear-splitting sounds. The masks are carved by craftsmen – see far left. Next to the carver, a mask painter at work (far right).

Südlich einer imaginären Linie von Ehingen an der Donau über Rottenburg am Neckar bis nach Offenburg ist die Fasnacht oder Fasnet eine mancherorts schon seit dem Mittelalter nachgewiesene Tradition, die in jeder Stadt und jedem Dorf auf unverwechselbare Art gefeiert wird. Die schwäbisch-alemannische Fasnacht hat mit dem rheinischen Karneval oder dem bayerischen Fasching wenig gemein. Hier, im Südwesten Deutschlands, gibt es weder das Funkenmariechen noch den Faschingsprinzen, dafür aber altüberlieferte Narrenfiguren mit kunstvoll gearbeiteten Masken und dem „Häs", dem Kostüm. Diese Narrentracht wird von den Vätern an die Söhne vererbt, neuerdings auch an die Töchter, denn es sabotieren immer mehr Mädchen das männliche Privileg, an der Fasnacht als Akteure teilnehmen zu dürfen. In diesem Sinne: Narri, Narro!

South of an imaginary line drawn from Ehingen on the Danube to Rottenburg on the Neckar and to Offenburg, the "Fasnacht" or "Fasnet" is a Mardi Gras tradition that in some places dates back to the Middle Ages. In every town and village, it takes on its own characteristic form. The Swabian-Alemannic Fasnacht is quite unlike the "Karneval" tradition on the Rhine or the Bavarian "Fasching". Here, in Southwestern Germany, there are no dancing girls or carnival princes, but traditional jester figures with artfully carved masks and "Häs", i.e. costumes. The fool's costumes are passed on from father to son, more recently also to daughters, since more and more girls have come to challenge the male privilege of playing an active part in the Fasnacht. In this vein: "Narri, Narro!"

Präg bei Gewitterstimmung: Die Ansammlung von Höfen in der Nähe von Schönau im Südschwarzwald sieht fast noch so aus, wie sie Hans Thoma 1898 gezeichnet hat.

Präg before a thunderstorm: This group of farms near Schönau in the southern part of the Black Forest appears today almost as on the picture painted by Hans Thoma in 1898.

35

Die Porphyrfelsen des Battert stehen eindrucksvoll über Baden-Baden. Das Massiv erhebt sich nur 2 km nördlich der Kurstadt und erfreut sich nach wie vor bei Bergsteigern und Kletterern großer Beliebtheit. Der Battert ist aber auch von Wanderern zu erreichen, über Treppen und Brücken in den Felsen und auf dem „Einsiedlerweg". Der Rundwanderweg berührt im Osten und im Norden Reste eines keltischen Ringwalls. Rechte Seite: Die Hexenlochmühle, im obersten Winkel des Tals der Wilden Gutach, Inbegriff der Schwarzwaldmühle. Über der kleinen Straße, die an ihr vorbeiführt, steigen Felsen und Schluchtwald beinahe senkrecht an, bilden gleichsam ein dunkelgrün-graues Tunnelgewölbe.

The Battert, a porphyry rock, towers imposingly above Baden-Baden. The massif is only two kilometers north of the spa and has always been very popular with rock climbers and mountaineers. Hikers can get to the top by way of stairs and bridges cut into the rock, or follow the so-called "Hermit's Path". The path describes a big circle, touching the remains of a celtic ring wall in the east and the north.
Right: The Hexenlochmühle in the uppermost corner of the Wild Gutach valley, the epitome of a Black Forest mill. Cliffs and wooded gorges rise up almost vertically along the small street beside it, forming a tunnel of dark green and grey.

Die Fächerstadt Karlsruhe – ein Tor zum Schwarzwald. Die ehemalige Residenz der Großherzöge von Baden und heutige Residenz des Rechts – in Karlsruhe befinden sich die höchsten deutschen Gerichte – ist städtebaulich so konzipiert, daß ihre Straßen fächergleich auf das Schloß zu laufen. In Karlsruhe, das am Rhein liegt, nahe der Pfalz, nahe Frankreich, breitet sich eine lebensfrohe Atmosphäre aus. Dazu passen so recht Gerichte aus dem Schwarzwald: Rehrücken Baden-Baden, im Bild ganz rechts, mit Weintrauben, Pfifferlingen, Eßkastanien und Williamsbirnen, Spätzle oder Butternudeln. Unten links, etwas deftiger, Schinken im Brotteig, mit gemischtem Kartoffel- und Gurkensalat. Rechts – ungewöhnlich und zunächst unverständlich – Scherben, eine regionale Bezeichnung für in Fett gebackene Fasnetsküchla, die nicht nur an der Fasnacht schmecken. Weltberühmt wurde die Schwarzwälder Kirschtorte. Kreierte ein Baden-Badener, ein Badenweiler, ein Freudenstädter oder ein Herrenalber Konditor diese verführerische Köstlichkeit? – Man weiß es nicht. Genießern ist das auch egal.

The fan-shaped town Karlsruhe – a gateway to the Black Forest. The onetime residence of the Great Dukes of Baden and modern residence of justice – the German supreme court resides at Karlsruhe – has been planned in the shape of a fan with all streets leading directly to the palace. Karlsruhe, situated on the Rhine near the Palatinate and France, exudes a bright, cheerful atmosphere. These impressions are enhanced by local dishes from the Black Forest: On the right, Saddle of Venison Baden-Baden Style, with grapes, chanterelles, chestnuts and Williams pears, served with Spätzle or buttered noodles. Below left, somewhat heartier, Ham Wrapped in Bread Dough with a potato-cucumber salad. Above left – unusual and quite incomprehensible at first – Scherben, i.e. shards, a regional name for deep-fried Fasnetsküchla, small shreds of dough. They are delicious, and not only at Mardi Gras. The Black Forest Gateau is famous all over the world. Was this sumptuous delicacy created by a pastry-cook from Baden-Baden, Badenweiler, Freudenstadt or Herrenalb? Nobody knows. Gourmets don't care anyway.

einen Tälern wachte
n Herz mir auf
❙ Leben, Deine Wellen
spielten mich ...
❙ Hölderlins Gedicht
❙ Neckar")
❙ Dichter wurde 1770 in Lauffen
❙ Neckar geboren, wuchs in
tingen auf, studierte in
ingen und starb dort auch
h langen Jahren im berühmt
rordenen Turm direkt überm
karufer.
, im Schwenninger Moos, aus
sen Wassern der ganz junge
kar gespeist wird, ist von
en noch längst nichts zu
en. Keiner hat seinen Lauf
ser beschrieben als Sebastian
❙er in seinem Gedicht „Dr
ker". Da heißt es am Schluß
r den aus dem Schwäbischen
menden ... was aber tuat der
mer? Er läuft schnurstracks
Badische nei - ond dort - vor
er Jomer - versäuft er sich em
❙!" - Was doch auf eine innige
undenheit zwischen
ttemberg und Baden
eßen läßt!

Das Neckartal

Der mit seinen Zuflüssen weit ins Land reichende Neckar ist bis zu seiner Einmündung in den Rhein schlechthin zum Strom der württembergischen Schwaben und Franken sowie der Kurpfälzer geworden. Er entspringt bei Schwenningen – dem württembergischen Teil der Doppelstadt Villingen-Schwenningen – in einem Quellmoor, dessen vielen kleinen Rinnsalen er sein Leben verdankt. Er bekommt sein Wasser dann aus Bächen und kleineren Flüssen, die auf einer Strecke von annähernd 400 km bis Mannheim zu ihm finden: der Enz etwa oder der Rems, dem Kocher oder der Jagst. Neckartal und Neckarland liegen zwischen dem Schwarzwald und der Schwäbischen Alb, bilden um und nördlich von Stuttgart einen großen Teil des Unterlands und werden dort von Hohenlohe und Kraichgau umrahmt. Mit seinem Unterlauf durchsägt der Fluß schließlich den Odenwald. Der Neckar läßt außerdem den Schönbuch links und den Schurwald rechts liegen, er gebärdet sich – wie alle Flüsse – eigenwillig, hat sich seinen Lauf in Jahrmillionen gesucht. Und er kann einiges aufweisen: stolze Städte und romantische Dörfer, Uferlandschaften mit Feldern, Äckern und Wiesen, mit Weinbergen und Felsformationen, andere mit Industrieanlagen und Kraftwerken. Teilweise zwang man ihn in sein Flußbett, teilweise ist er kanalisiert, wiewohl er in jüngster Zeit hier und da auch renaturiert wird.

Zum Neckar gehören die Fasnacht um Rottweil, der Bischof von Rottenburg, die Universität in Tübingen, es gehören zu ihm erhalten gebliebene altehrwürdige Städte wie Esslingen, das Volksfest in Cannstatt, Schiller in Marbach, das große Barockschloß in Ludwigsburg, der Schäferlauf in Markgröningen, das Käthchen von Heilbronn, das Salz unter Friedrichshall, die Türme in Wimpfen, das Falkennest auf Guttenberg, die Schiffer in Haßmersheim, Eberbach, das dem Fabulierer Mark Twain in unauslöschlicher Erinnerung blieb, und schließlich, sozusagen als Krönung, Heidelberg, „die Schöne", allen Reisenden aus Amerika und Japan ein Inbegriff von „merry old Germany". – Seine Eigenwilligkeit, zugegeben, leidet letztlich doch einigermaßen. Der Neckar ergießt sich in den Rhein, bei Mannheim verläßt ihn seine Kraft, doch auch dazu paßt ein Dichterwort.

The Neckar Valley

The Neckar, with its affluents reaching deep into the country-side, may be considered the home river of all Württemberg Swabians, Franconians and inhabitants of the Electoral Palatinate. It originates near Schwenningen – the Württemberg part of the double-town Villingen-Schwenningen –, owing its existence to the many tiny runs of a boggy headwaters area. Subsequently, on its course of more than 400 kilometers to Mannheim, it receives the waters of a multitude of brooks and small streams: of the Enz or the Rems, for example, or the Kocher and the Jagst. The Neckar valley or region separates the Black Forest from the Schwäbische Alb mountains, forming a great part of the lowlands around and to the north of Stuttgart, where it borders the Hohenlohe and Kraichgau regions. Further on, the lower part of the river finally cuts through the Odenwald, ignoring both the Schönbuch hills on the left and the Schurwald on the right. It runs quite wilfully, like all rivers, having found its way in the course of millions of years, and has a great deal to show for it: proud towns and romantic villages as well as river banks bordering fields, pastures and meadows, vineyards and rock formations, but also built up with industrial sites and power plants. In some parts, the river has been channeled or forced to stay in its bed, although of late it has been returned to its original state in certain areas.

The Neckar stands for "Fasnacht", the Mardi Gras tradition at Rottweil, the Bishop of Rottenburg, the University of Tübingen, but also for time-honored, well-preserved towns like Esslingen, the folk festival at Cannstatt, Schiller at Marbach, the great baroque palace at Ludwigsburg, the shepherds' race at Markgröningen, the literary figure "Käthchen of Heilbronn", the salt beneath Friedrichshall, the towers of Wimpfen, the falcon eyrie on Guttenberg, the boatmen in Haßmersheim, as well as Eberbach, forever in the memory of the storyteller Mark Twain, and finally, for Heidelberg, "the beautiful city", the epitome of „merry old Germany" for many a traveler from America and Japan. The river's wilfulness, however, admittedly, mellows a little in the end. It flows into the Rhine at Mannheim, all its strength exhausted, for which another poet found fitting words.

In your valleys my heart opened up
to life, your waves gently stroking me ...
(from the poem „The Neckar" by Hölderlin)
The poet was born in 1770 at Lauffen on the Neckar, grew up at Nürtingen and studied at Tübingen where he later also died, in the now famous tower directly above the banks of the Neckar. Here, in the Schwenninger Moos, the headwaters area of the Neckar, waves are nowhere to be seen yet. Nobody has described its course better than Sebastian Blau in his poem "Dr Necker". His final words about the river, which originates in Swabia, are as follows: "But where does the rover go? It runs straight across the Baden line – and there – for despair and woe – it drowns itself in the Rhine!" Quite an adequate description of the tender bonds between Württemberg and Baden.

Oben: Ein Glockengießer bei der Feinarbeit. Daneben: Trachten- träger von der Baar, einer kargen Landschaft mit rauhem Klima. Das Bauernleben dort war immer be- sonders hart und zwang zur Be- scheidenheit; trotzdem wirkt die Sonntagstracht recht aufwendig. Unten: Auf der Baar wird viel Getreide angepflanzt. So gab es auch viele Mühlen, von denen sich einige halten konnten, wie über- haupt am Lauf des Neckar. Hier der Müller in der Talmühle von Dauchingen. Rechte Seite: Ritterrüstungen werden gefertigt, nicht für die Schlacht, sondern für Museen als Anschauungsobjekte.

Far left: A bell founder doing o work. Next to it: People in the traditional costume of the Baa barren landscape with a harsh climate. Peasants have always a hard life there, with modesty being a necessity. Nevertheless the traditional sunday costume makes quite a costly impressio Below: Grains are the main crop the Baar, supporting a great number of mills, some of which like elsewhere on the Neckar – run today. The picture shows th miller of the Talmühle mill at Dauchingen. Right: Fashioning knight's armour, not for battle but for museums and illustratic purposes.

Am Neckar hat die Kunst des Handwerks Tradition. Dabei dürfen wir nicht nur an die Ortschaften unmittelbar an den Ufern des Flusses denken, sondern auch an die im Um- und Hinterland, zum Schwarzwald und zur Alb hin. Präzise, von Generation zu Generation überlieferte Handarbeit ließ denn auch eine ebenso genau und pünktlich herstellende Industrie entstehen. Sie blühte durch die Handwerkskunst auf. Beide – Handwerk und Industrie – ergänzen sich noch heute.

The crafts have a long tradition on the Neckar. This is not only true for the villages directly on the banks of the river but also for those in the region and the hinterland, towards the Black Forest and the Alb. A tradition of diligence in handicrafts passed on from generation to generation, over time developed into a booming manufacturing industry characterized by the same precision and exactitude. Even today, the crafts and industries compliment each other.

Wer einmal dabei war, kann süchtig werden: nach dem Rottweiler Narrensprung, einem ursprünglichen, wilden, aufwühlenden Fasnachts-Ereignis, das von Mal zu Mal mehr fasziniert. Schon lang sind deswegen die Rottweiler Narren nicht mehr unter sich, es kommen Zünfte und Besucher von nah und fern. Der Narrensprung, ein turbulenter Umzug durch die Straßen und Gassen der ehemaligen Reichsstadt, vorbei an erkergeschmückten Häuserzeilen, gilt als eine der reizvollsten Volksfasnachten in Europa. Der Brauch stammt aus dem 16. Jahrhundert. Das Bild läßt erkennen, daß sich Gschellnarren, Federahannes und Schantle – Rottweiler Fasnachtsfiguren – auch durch Regen nicht von ihrem tollen Treiben abhalten lassen. Und die Zuschauer spannen eben ihre Regenschirme auf.

Blick von Mannheim nach Ludwigshafen, im Hintergrund der Pfälzer Wald (rechts). Mannheim wurde aus strategischen Gründen in den Flußwinkel zwischen Rhein und Neckar gedrängt. 1606 begann der Bau der Stadt, die ähnlich wie Karlsruhe nach geometrischen Gesichtspunkten angelegt wurde. Starke Akzente – Schloß, Altes Rathaus, Jesuitenkirche – charakterisieren noch immer den alten barocken Baubestand. Im Mannheimer Nationaltheater wurden Schillers „Räuber" uraufgeführt. Längst ist Mannheim eine der bedeutendsten Industriestädte in Baden-Württemberg geworden. Rechte Seite: die Moschee im Schwetzinger Schloßpark. Kurfürst Carl Theodor von der Pfalz, der in Mannheim residierte, baute Schwetzingen zu seinem Sommersitz aus. Einst sah Voltaire im bezaubernden Schloßtheater französische Aufführungen, heute finden hier jeden Sommer Festspiele statt. Die Moschee entsprang einer Laune des Bauherrn, sie war nie ein Gebetshaus für Moslems, sondern diente, wie die Tempel im Park, der Staffage.

A view from Mannheim to Ludwigshafen, in the background the Pfälzer Wald forest (left). Mannheim was pressed into the angle formed by Rhine and Neckar for strategic reasons. Construction work for the city, which, like Karlsruhe, was built according to a geometric pattern, began in 1606. Baroque buildings such as the palace, the old city hall and the Jesuitenkirche church still characterize the old town. The first performance of Schiller's drama "Die Räuber" took place at the Mannheim National Theater. Today, Mannheim is one of the most industrialized cities in Baden-Württemberg. Right: The mosque in the palace gardens at Schwetzingen. Elector Carl Theodor of the Palatinate, who resided at Mannheim, chose Schwetzingen for his summer residence. The magnificent palace theater, where Voltaire once watched French plays, is now the site of an annual summer festival. The mosque was built on a whim of the elector and never served as a place for Muslim prayer. It was meant only for show, as was the temple in the park.

Der Rhein als Flußgott im Großen Weiher von Schwetzingen. Die Zierbauten im Park – Tempel des Apollo, des Merkur oder der Minerva, das Römische Wasserkastell, das Rondell der wasserspeienden Vögel und andere mehr – entstammen der gleichen Geisteshaltung: dem sentimentalen Naturempfinden im ausklingenden Barock.

Warum nicht einmal Odenwälder Spezialitäten? Die Kartoffelsuppe etwa (rechts), eine Variante mit Kartoffelhörnchen, einem Gebäck aus dem Mehl der geriebenen Knolle, in das Zwetschgenmus gegeben wird – kompakt und sättigend! Ganz anders (darunter) Forellen in feinem Kräuterrahm. Die Odenwaldforelle wird von jedem Küchenchef nach seiner Art zubereitet. Dann natürlich der Spargel, wobei es nicht unbedingt der berühmte Schwetzinger sein muß. Hier (unten rechts) Spargel mit „Strübli" und Schinken. Strübli – Pfannkuchen – und rohen oder gekochten Schinken gibt es das ganze Jahr, frischen Stangenspargel nur im Frühjahr. Als Vorspeise, zwischendrin oder zum guten Schluß einen Odenwälder Zwiwwelkuche (Zwiebelkuchen, ganz rechts oben) und dazu einen kräftigen, herben Apfelwein, einen „Ebbelwoi" – da kommt der Appetit von allein.

The Rhine as a river deity in the great pond at Schwetzingen. All of the ornamental buildings in the park – the temples of Apollo, Mercury or Minerva, the Roman water citadel, the circle of water-spouting birds, among other things – express the sentimental perception of nature in the late Baroque.

Why not try specialties from the Odenwald region? Potato Soup for instance (above left), a version with Potato Croissants, pastries made from the flour of the grated tuber mixed with plum sauce – both solid and filling! Below, next to it, but quite different: Trout in a Fine Herbed Cream Sauce. Every chef has his own recipe for Odenwald trout. And asparagus, of course, although they do not necessarily have to come from Schwetzingen. Below left, asparagus with "Strübli" and ham. "Strübli" – pancakes – served with raw or cooked ham, are available all year round, asparagus only in late spring. Finally, an Odenwald "Zwiwwelkuche" (onion tarte), and to go with it a rich, dry apple cider – so-called "Ebbelwoi" –, a mouthwatering sight.

71

Das Hohenloher Land

Sonderbar, ein Hesse hat in Franken den „schwäbischen Gruß" erfunden. Goethe läßt in seinem Ritterschauspiel Götz von Berlichingen die weltberühmte Aufforderung kundtun, ihn „hinten zu lecken". War auch der große Dichter der weitverbreiteten Meinung, die Heimat des Götz, des Ritters mit der eisernen Hand, liege in Schwaben? Sicher nicht, denn Goethe selbst sprach ja nie vom „schwäbischen Gruß".

Hohenlohe ist fränkisch und gehört erst seit 1806 zum damaligen Württemberg, das durch Napoleon zum Königreich erhoben worden war – sehr zum Ärger der bis dahin regierenden Fürsten von Hohenlohe. Das ändert nichts daran, daß der fränkische Teil Baden-Württembergs eigentlich schon südlich von Heilbronn beginnt. Der Wald zwischen der Rems und den Waldenburger Bergen heißt deshalb auch „Schwäbisch-Fränkischer Wald". Hinter ihm breitet sich Franken aus – oder besser, nördlich von ihm, um nicht in den Verdacht zu geraten, die Hohenloher als „hinterwäldlerisch" zu bezeichnen. Das sind sie ganz bestimmt nicht, sie sind eher hellwach, knitz, nicht selten „schlitzöhrig", wie man zu Menschen sagt, die die Fähigkeit besitzen, andere an der Nase herumzuführen. Vor allem aber sind sie aufgeschlossen, freundlich und fast so köstlich wie der Wein, den sie erzeugen. Kein Wunder, bei der Landschaft, in der sie leben, in einer Welt alter Bauernsiedlungen und einer adligen Welt vieler Schlösser und Burgen. Das eine ergänzt das andere. Hinzu kommen prächtige Klöster, heilige Kapellen, stolze Städte.

Wer im Hohenlohischen unterwegs ist, kommt von Adelssitz zu Adelssitz, man spürt direkt, wie fürstlich-freiherrlich das Land geprägt ist. Fast jedes Städtchen war mal Residenz, was zum einen beweist, daß das Geschlecht der Hohenlohe weitverzweigt ist – mit Bindungen in alle Welt, zum anderen aber auch, daß Napoleon mit der Bereinigung der Duodezherrschaften gar nicht so unrecht hatte. Doch das ist Geschichte. Es gilt, was ein Reiseschriftsteller seiner Zeit, Karl Julius Weber, 1826 geschrieben hat: „Das Fürstentum Hohenlohe ist einer der wertvollsten Edelsteine in Württembergs Krone, es hat alles aufzuweisen, was man billigerweise wünschen kann."

The Hohenlohe Region

Astonishingly enough, a native of Hesse invented the so-called "Swabian greeting", and in Franconia. In his drama, Goethe had his knight Götz of Berlichingen invite his enemies "to kiss his behind." Could the great poet have been harboring the popular misconception that the home of Götz, the knight with the iron fist, was in Swabia? Unlikely, since Goethe himself never called it "Swabian greeting."

Hohenlohe belongs to Franconia and only became part of what was then known as Württemberg in 1806, when Napoleon made it a kingdom – an action that quite aggravated the formerly ruling princes of Hohenlohe. But this does not change the fact that the Franconian part of Baden-Württemberg really already begins south of Heilbronn. Thus, the forest between the Rems and the Waldenburger Berge is called "Swabian-Franconian Forest." Behind it lies Franconia, or better to the north of it, since we do not want to be accused of calling the inhabitants of Hohenlohe backwards. And far from it they are, on the contrary, they are quite alert, smart or even "cheeky", as people who know how to pull the wool over the eyes of others are generally called. Above all, they are open-minded and friendly and almost as special as the wine they produce. Small miracle, considering the surroundings in which they live: Their world includes both old rural hamlets and noble castles and palaces, one complementing the other. Magnificent monasteries, holy chapels, proud towns: Travelers in the Hohenlohe region encounter manor after manor, the princely character of the land is much in evidence. Almost every town was once a residence, for one illustrating the fact that the Hohenlohe dynasty has numerous branches – with ties to the whole world – but also that Napoleon's abolishing of petty principalities was not such a bad idea after all. This is history, however. And the words of the travel author Karl Julius Weber from 1826 are still valid today: "The principality Hohenlohe is one of the most precious gems in Württemberg's crown – it has everything one could reasonably wish for."

Bild links: Burg und Kloster, Kirche und Chorherrenstift – all dies hat die Comburg schon erlebt. Die ursprüngliche Benediktiner-Abtei erhebt sich als einst wehrhaft umringte Klosterstadt auf einem Hügel über dem Kochertal bei Schwäbisch Hall. Seit dem 10. Jahrhundert saßen dort die fränkischen Grafen von Comburg. 1802 wurde das Kloster aufgelöst, die Kirche dient seitdem als katholische Pfarrkirche.
Bild rechts: Als Hohenlohe 1806 durch die napoleonische Neuordnung zu Württemberg geschlagen wurde, brachten die schwäbischen Beamten an möglichst vielen Stellen das Wappen ihres Königs an. Auf der Jagstbrücke von Hohebach ließen sie eine Art Triumphsäule errichten, weil hier eine neue Straße – die heutige Bundesstraße 19 – über die Jagst ging. Rund 150 Jahre danach war das nicht mehr so wichtig, und der ehemalige Pfarrer von Bächlingen und Archivar der Fürsten von Hohenlohe-Langenburg, Rudolf Schlauch, schwärmte von diesem liebenswerten Land an Kocher, Jagst und Tauber, auf dessen Straßen „die alten Kaiser ritten, die Minnesänger sangen und die Bauern heute noch von Markt zu Markt fahren wie eh und je, auf Straßen, auf denen im Sommer die Garbenwagen schwanken und im Herbst die Traubenbottiche zur Kelter geführt werden."

Left: Castle and monastery, church and canon chapter – Comburg has been all of it. Originally an abbey of the Benedictine order, the formerly circumvallated monastery town presides on a hill above the Kocher valley near Schwäbisch Hall. In the 10th century, it became the seat of the Franconian counts of Comburg. In 1802, the monastery was disbanded; the church has since served as a catholic parish church.
Above: After the Napoleonic reforms, when Hohenlohe became part of Württemberg, Swabian civil servants applied the coat of arms of their king to as many surfaces as possible. On the occasion of the opening of a new road across the river – today's federal route 19 – a kind of triumphal column was erected on the bridge across the Jagst at Hohebach. Nowadays, the former priest of Bächlingen and archivist of the princes of Hohenlohe-Langenburg, Rudolf Schlauch, is just as enthusiastic about this lovely region between Kocher, Jagst and Tauber, whose roads have carried "emperors of old and singing minstrels, and whose peasants still go from market to market as in the days of yore, on streets where one encounters wobbling wagons with sheaves of grain in summer and vats full of grapes ready for pressing in fall.

Schwäbisch Hall. Die schöne Stadt am Kocher hat eine reiche Geschichte und war einst auch eine wahrhaft reiche Stadt, begründet durch ein großes Territorium, das zu ihr gehörte, und durch die Salzvorkommen. An diese erinnern die jährlich an Pfingsten gefeierten Feste der Salzsieder, die fast so bekannt sind wie die Freilichtspiele auf der gewaltigen Treppe der Michaelskirche. Ursprünglich wurde dort der „Jedermann" aufgeführt, inzwischen wird jegliches Theater gemacht, vom Schauspiel bis zur Operette und zum Musical. Hall war freie Reichsstadt, in Hall wurde der „Häller" geprägt, eine Münze, die die Redensart „vom letzten Heller" begründete. Erst im Mittelalter gaben sich die einst staufischen Haller den Beinamen „Schwäbisch". Das ändert nichts daran, daß sie Franken sind und zu den Hohenlohern gehören.

Schwäbisch Hall. This handsome town on the Kocher may look back on a lively history. It once was a truly wealthy city due to its large territory and the salt mines it owned. The saltboilers' festival, which takes place every year at Pentecost, serves as a reminder. It is almost as well-known as the open air festival on the huge stairway of St. Michael's. Originally, the play performed was "Everyman", but nowadays it includes a whole range of theater performances, from dramas to operettas to musicals. Hall was a free city, with the right to mint "Häller", a coin which gave rise to the phrase about "the last Heller", i.e. penny. The city of Hall, formerly part of Staufen, only added the epithet "Swabian" to its name in the Middle Ages. This does not change the fact that it is in Franconia, belonging to Hohenlohe.

Links Weinberge bei Heuholz. Am Westhang der Waldenburger Berge wachsen gehaltvolle Weine, die freilich meist von den Hohenlohern selbst getrunken werden. Oben die reizvolle Silhouette des alten Residenzstädtchens Waldenburg, dessen Türme und Stadtmauern die Zerstörungen in den letzten Tagen des Zweiten Weltkriegs überstanden. Der große Rest von Waldenburg indes mußte wiederaufgebaut werden. Unten Abendstimmung bei der Kochermühle in Forchtenberg.

Far left, vineyards near Heuholz. The western slope of the Waldenburg mountains produces strong wines, most of which are consumed by the inhabitants of Hohenlohe themselves, however. Above, the charming skyline of the old residence town Waldenburg, whose towers and walls survived the devastations of the closing days of World War II. Most of Waldenburg's remaining buildings had to be rebuilt. Below, evening scene near the Kochermühle mill at Forchtenberg.

Viele stilvolle Bauten aus vergangenen Jahrhunderten schmücken das winkelige, von Gassen durchzogene Künzelsau, wie hier im sogenannten Honigzipfel. Um den Stadtkern und auf der Höhe in Gaisbach und Garnberg haben sich aber auch weltbekannte Betriebe angesiedelt, so daß die Verwaltungs- und Schulstadt durchaus als Wirtschaftszentrum bezeichnet werden kann. Zu den baulichen Kostbarkeiten gehören das Fachwerk-Rathaus, das aus einer Wasserburg hervorgegangene Schloß, der Comburger Pfleghof und das Würzburger Haus. Wunderschön ist die Johannesapotheke von 1773. Deren Rokokoschnitzwerk stammt aus der Werkstatt der Schreiner- und Bildhauerfamilie Sommer, die sich einer bodenständigen Handwerkskunst verpflichtet fühlte.

Numerous buildings in the styles of past centuries, lining crooked alleyways, characterize Künzelsau, for example here, at the so-called "Honigzipfel". However, the center of town and the hills Gaisbach and Garnberg also accomodate numerous firms that are active worldwide. Thus, the administrative and educational town may well be called an economic center. The gems among the buildings include the half-timber city hall, the palace formerly a moat-encircled castle, the so-called Comburg Pfleghof and the Würzburg House. The marvelous pharmacy Johannesapotheke dates from 1773. Its rococo carvings were done by the Sommer family, a dynasty of carpenters and sculptors dedicated to the local crafts.

as Pfedelbacher Faß verheißt
icht nur guten Wein in großen
ebinden, es vermittelt auch den
urch Weingenuß gesegneten
rohsinn der Hohenloher.
echts das Schloß in Öhringen,
om Hofgarten her gesehen. Im
hemaligen Schloß der Hohen-
oher Fürsten sind heute die Amts-
äume des Rathauses unterge-
racht, in seinem Keller lagern die
Weine des fürstlichen Gutes. Auch
ier befindet sich ein großes Faß,
as der Dichter Nikolaus Lenau
oetisch verewigt hat. Hinter dem
chloß erhebt sich die Stiftskirche,
eren Bau im 11. Jahrhundert be-
onnen wurde.

The "Pfedelbacher Barrel" not only
promises excellent wine in large
quantities, but also provides the
inhabitants of Hohenlohe with
wine-inspired merriment.
On the left, the palace at
Öhringen, seen from the Hofgarten.
The former palace of the princes
of Hohenlohe now houses munici-
pal administrative offices, its cellar
the wines of the princely estate
and another large barrel, immortalized by the poet Nikolaus Lenau.
In the background the Stiftskirche,
a church whose foundations were
laid in the 11th century.

er Reiz der Hohenloher Land-
haft liegt im Wechsel tiefer
ußtäler und weiter Hochebenen,
e, wie links zu sehen, stets leicht
ewellt sind. Oben das Kloster
höntal an der Jagst, Wirkungs-
ätte des geistreichen Abts
enedikt Knittel, dem die Knittel-
rse zu verdanken sind. Unten
r Innenhof der Götzenburg in
gsthausen, in der Goethes „Götz
on Berlichingen" aufgeführt wird.

The charm of the Hohenlohe landscape lies in the alternation of
deeply cut river valleys and wide
high plains with soft slopes, as
seen on the picture on the left.
Above, the monastery Schöntal on
the Jagst, domain of the witty
abbot Benedikt Knittel, who was
famous for his rhyming iambs.
Below, a performance of Goethe's
drama Götz of Berlichingen in the
courtyard of the original Götz
castle at Jagsthausen.

Mitten in der freien Landschaft erhebt sich zwischen Gröningen und Wallhausen die Anhäuser Mauer, die einstmals die nördliche Seitenwand eines Chores in einem ansehnlichen Kloster war. Während des Bauernkriegs herrschte dort ein verhaßter Abt, dem die Aufständischen sein Kloster in Brand steckten.
Rechte Seite: Das Schloß der Hohenloher Linie Langenburg in Langenburg. Hoch über der Jagst eröffnen sich nicht nur weite Ausblicke auf das Flußtal und das Land ringsum, sondern auch Einblicke in die Vergangenheit. Neben einem Besuch der Waffensammlung ist einer im Automuseum empfehlenswert. Die Langenburger sind Verwandte des englischen Königshauses, weshalb die Queen schon etliche Male im Schloß war – unbemerkt von der Öffentlichkeit.

Between Gröningen and Wallhausen, the so-called Anhäuser Wall, formerly the northern chancel wall of a stately monastery, rises freely from the landscape. Ruled by an odious abbot at the time of the uprisings in the 16th century, it was set on fire by rebellious peasants.
Right: The palace of the Hohenlohe-Langenburg line at Langenburg. High above the Jagst, visitors not only have a grand view over the river valley, but may also catch a glimpse of the past: Both armour and car museum are well worth seeing. The Langenburg line is related to the House of Windsor, and the Queen has been a guest at the castle several times – largely unnoticed by the public.

Imposant der Rittersaal im Schloß zu Weikersheim. Einst konnte in ihn hoch zu Roß hineingeritten werden. Aus der Zeit um 1600 gibt es kaum einen Saal, der so gut erhalten geblieben ist.
Oben Tauberbischofsheim mit dem Kurmainzischen Schloß. In der Stadt an der Tauber befindet sich das Trainingszentrum der deutschen Weltklasse-Fechter.

The knight's hall of the castle at Weikersheim, which could be entered by knights on horseback. There are very few halls from the time around 1600 which are so well preserved.
Above, Tauberbischofsheim and Kurmainz Palace. The town on the Tauber is the home of the training center for the world-class German fencing team.

Museen zeugen von der Hohenloher Bauernkultur und vom Leben in den Dörfern, wie hier im Freilandmuseum Wackershofen bei Schwäbisch Hall: Dort werden beinahe ausnahmslos Häuser gezeigt, die in der weiteren Umgebung abgetragen – dabei oft vor dem Untergang gerettet – und in passenden Ensembles wieder aufgebaut wurden.

Museums like the open-air museum Wackershofen near Schwäbisch Hall document rural culture and village life in the Hohenlohe region. The houses shown there are all from the region, dismantled at their original sites – which often saved them from ruin – and rebuilt in suitable groups.

Hohenlohisch-fränkische Gerichte mit einem deutlichen Fingerzeig ins Schwäbische, speziell auf die Schwäbische Alb: Die Geschmälzte Brotsuppe (oben) mit Zwiebel, magerem Rauchspeck, Schweineschmalz, Weiß- und Graubrot sowie als Einlage Ei und etwas Leber- sprich Fleischkäse wird der Alb zu- geschrieben. Resteverwertung in Form köstlicher Brotsuppen findet man indes häufig, so oder abge- wandelt, meist mit nur wenigen Zutaten, beispielsweise in den Gebirgen Bayerns, Österreichs oder der Schweiz. Die Grünkernküchle (unten links) erinnern daran, daß im Nordosten von Baden-Würt- temberg verhältnismäßig viel Dinkel oder seine unreif geerntete Variante Grünkern angebaut wird. Und der Herbstblootz mit Äpfeln und Birnen ist nur eine Sorte dieses vielseitigen, eher dünnen Kuchens, den man nach Herzens- lust salzig oder süß machen und mit allem Möglichen – Zwiebeln, Schnittlauch, Speck, Rahm oder Zwetschgen – belegen kann.

Dishes from the Franconian Hohenlohe region with a distinctly Swabian touch: Bread Soup With A Bread Crumb Topping (above), featuring onions, lean bacon, lard, white bread and rye bread as well as a garnish of eggs and pieces of bologna, is said to originate from the Schwäbische Alb mountains. However, delicious bread soups as a means of using up leftovers, in this or a slightly different form, are popular elsewhere, too, for example in the mountainous regions of Bavaria, Austria or Switzerland. Green Spelt Burgers (bottom left) are a reminder that quite a lot of spelt or its variant green spelt, which is picked before ripening, is cultivated in the northeastern part of Baden-Würt- temberg. Finally, Fall Tarte With Apples and Pears is only one version of that versatile, thin cake, which may be savory or sweet according to the cook's mood, and whose toppings may include any- thing from onions, chives, bacon and cream to plums.

Die Schwäbische Alb

„Droba uf dr rauha Alb, wie machen's da die Bauern all? – Sie laufen die Furchen auf und ab und fluchen die Sterne von Himmel herab …" Das Volkslied, das beim Singen fröhlich klingt, weil immer wieder ein „Jupheidi" eingefügt wird und weil die Melodie lustig ist, hat sein Entstehen sicher einem Galgenhumor zu verdanken. Die Bauern auf der Alb hatten es immer schwer, früher viel mehr als heute, hatten sie doch auf ihren Äckern oft mehr Steine als Kartoffeln. Deswegen verließen sie sich nicht auf die Landwirtschaft alleine, die Älbler wurden, als dies möglich war, zu Handwerkern und Erfindern, zu Arbeitern und Industriellen. Das ist die eine, die soziologische, die wirtschaftliche Seite der Alb. Es gibt noch so manche andere, vor allem natürlich die geologische, die landschaftliche.

Wer im Brockhaus von 1923 nachschlägt, um etwas über die Schwäbische Alb zu erfahren, findet lediglich den Hinweis auf die „Rauhe Alb". Da verrät das Lexikon, das Mittelgebirge sei der breiteste Teil des Schwäbischen Jura, bestehe aus weißen, durchlässigen Malmkalken, habe einen Steilabfall („Albtrauf") nach Nordwesten und eine Abdachung zur Donau hin sowie zahlreiche vulkanische Durchbrüche aus der Tertiärzeit. Diesen wenigen Angaben ist hinzuzufügen, daß die Alb zum großen Jurabogen gehört, der sich vom Genfer See durch die Schweiz bis zur Grenze Tschechiens hinzieht. So reicht der schwäbische Teil vom Rheinfall bei Schaffhausen bis zum Ries bei Nördlingen.

Auf der Alb – der größten Karstlandschaft Deutschlands – streiten sich Neckar und Donau, deren Ursprünge nahe beieinander liegen, um das so knappe, kostbare Wasser. Dieses verschwindet, wie von einem Schwamm aufgesogen, in Irrgärten von Höhlen, Gängen und Klüften. Erst nach 1871, als der Mensch mit Hilfe der Technik die Albwasserversorgung schuf, wurden die größten Nöte behoben, wurde Wasser aus tiefer verlaufenden Flüssen auf die Hochflächen gepumpt.

Darüber hinaus hat die Alb ihre schöne Seite, sie gilt als unvergleichliches Wanderparadies: mit weiten Ausblicken ins Unterland und zu Alpengipfeln, mit Wacholderheiden, Schafherden, Streuobstwiesen und Pferdekoppeln, reizvollen Dörfern und Städten.

The Schwäbische Alb Mountains

"Up on the rough Alb mountains, what do the peasants do? – They run the furrows up and down and curse all the stars in the sky …" The folk song with the cheerful melody and its occasional addition of the nonsensical burden "Juppheidi" must owe its existence to a rather grim kind of humor. The farmers on the Alb always had a hard life, even more so in the past, with their fields frequently yielding more stones than potatoes. Since they could not rely on agriculture alone, the inhabitants of the Alb became craftsmen and inventors, workers and entrepreneurs whenever the possibility presented itself. This is only one – the sociological – aspect of the Alb. There are others, too, above all the geological and topographical one, of course.

If one consults the 1923 edition of the Brockhaus encyclopedia about the Alb, the only entry to be found is „Rough Alb." There, the region is classified as an area of highlands, with soil consisting of white, permeable Jurassic limestones, a steep decline towards the northwest ("Albtrauf") and a slant towards the Danube, as well as several volcanic break–throughs from the Tertiary. One might add that the Alb belongs to the great Jurassic arch extending from Lake Geneva through Switzerland all the way to the Czech border. The Swabian part encompasses the stretch from the Rhine Falls near Schaffhausen to the Ries near Nördlingen.

On the Alb – the largest German karst landscape –, the Neckar and the Danube, whose sources are close together, compete for water, a scarce and precious commodity. Water disappears, as if absorbed by sponge, in a labyrinth of caves, passages and gorges. The most dire water shortages were alleviated only after 1871, when people were able to supply water to the Alb with the help of new technology, and water from rivers running on a lower level could be pumped up to the highlands.

Yet, the Alb also has its beautiful aspects: With its wide views over the lowlands and onto the peaks of the Alps, its juniper heath, flocks of sheep, meadows of fruit trees, strings of horses and charming villages and towns, it is an unique paradise for hikers.

Here, in the Wen valley between Steinheim am Albuch and Bartholomä, ancient landscape formations may be explored on an easy walk (left). The path runs through a dry valley framed by mighty trees and bizarre dolomite rocks. One section is called "sea of rocks", an epithet appropriate for many a "wilderness" in the Schwäbische Alb mountains.
The small picture on the right shows the plant that has come to be a symbol for the Schwäbische Alb – a plant that thrives on the heath with its flocks of sheep and dry, stony soil. A member of the composite flower family, it is known by many names, the most fitting being carline thistle. Carline thistles like it warm. The white outer petals of the flowers open up in dry air and close when it is moist, giving rise to another of its names: "weather thistle".

Hier wird der Spaziergang zu einem Urwelt-Erlebnis: im Wental zwischen Steinheim am Albuch und Bartholomä (links). Der Weg führt durch ein Trockental, das von mächtigen Bäumen und bizarren Dolomitfelsen gesäumt wird. Ein Abschnitt trägt den für so manche „Wildnis" auf der Alb zutreffenden Namen „Felsenmeer".
Das kleine Bild rechts zeigt die Symbolpflanze der Schwäbischen Alb, die die dortigen Heiden und Schafe liebt, mit trockenem, steinigem Boden, eine Pflanze aus der Familie der Korbblütengewächse, die verschiedene Namen hat: Große Eberwurz, Stengellose Eberwurz, Wetterdistel und Silberdistel. Letzterer ziemt ihr wohl am ehesten. Die Silberdistel hat's gerne warm. Bei trockener Luft spreizen sich die weißen Hüllblätter der Blüten auseinander, bei feuchter bewegen sie sich nach innen. Daher Wetterdistel.

Hoch über dem oberen Donautal (rechts) ragt zwischen Fridingen und Beuron ein mächtiges Steingebilde, das einer Plastik gleicht, nahe dem Stiegelesfels auf. Wollte sich hier die Natur künstlerisch betätigen und das Abbild eines alten Menschen schaffen, den die grandiose Landschaft beeindruckt? Beim Stichwort Beuron sei darauf hingewiesen, daß hier eine der wenigen Erzabteien des Ordens der Benediktiner besteht, in der auch international beachtete wissenschaftliche Arbeit betrieben wird.

Auf der rechten Seite Schloß Lichtenstein über dem Echaztal. 1840/41 ließ sie Graf Wilhelm von Württemberg als „eine deutsche Ritterburg im edelsten Sinne des Mittelalters" errichten. Fast kitschig schön, gilt sie, auch in Erinnerung an den gleichnamigen Roman von Wilhelm Hauff, als ein historisches Wahrzeichen der Alb.

High above the upper Danube valley (left) between Fridingen and Beuron, an imposing formation of rock resembling a sculpture rises up near the Stiegelesfels rock. Was it that nature meant to be creative here and shape the likeness of an ancient man contemplating the grandiose landscape? Beuron, on the other hand, is the site of one of the few abbeys of the Benedictine order sustaining scholarly work of international importance.

On the right, Lichtenstein Castle above the Echaztal. Count Wilhelm of Württemberg had the castle built in 1840/41 as a "German knight's castle according to the most noble medieval ideals". A landmark of the Alb, its almost kitschy prettiness was immortalized in the novel of the same name by Wilhelm Hauff.

en Kornbühl (886 m) bei Salmen-
ngen auf dem Heufeld (links)
rönt eine Wallfahrtskapelle. Ein
tationenweg führt zu ihr hinauf.
er Kornbühl gehört wie der
ternberg, der Gönninger Roßberg
nd der Bolberg zu dem Kuppen-
elief der Alb, das zu ihren geolo-
ischen Besonderheiten zählt.
echts eine typische Wacholder-
eide bei Mahlstetten auf dem
roßen Heuberg.

A pilgrim's chapel crowns the
Kornbühl (886 m) near Salmen-
dingen auf dem Heufeld (far left).
A path with pilgrimage stations
leads up to it. The Kornbühl, along
with the Sternberg, the Gönninger
Roßberg and the Bolberg mountains, forms part of the relief of
knolls, a special geological feature
of the Alb region.
On the left, a typical juniper heath
near Mahlstetten on the Großen
Heuberg.

Nur an wenigen Stellen im Land gibt es echte Naturlandschaften, beispielsweise elsen oder Moore. Selbst seit Jahrzehnten der Nutzung entzogene Bannwälder oder eschützte Flußauen sind irgendwann vom Menschen geformt, mindestens geprägt orden. Erst recht gilt das für solch eine überlieferte Kulturlandschaft wie die Vacholderheide: Hier weiden die Herden der Schäfer, sorgen durch regelmäßigen esuch dafür, daß das magere Gras kurz gehalten, Busch- und Baumwuchs zurück-edrängt wird. Hier fühlen sich auch Wanderer und Spaziergänger wohl, und wenn im Vinter genug Schnee liegt, kommen die Skilangläufer. Ziehen keine Schäfer mehr, so nuß man regelmäßig mähen und auslichten.

Genuine natural formations like rocks and moors a rare in this region. Even woods that have not been used for forestry purposes for centuries and protected lowland meadows were once formed, or at least transformed, by man. This is especial-ly true for such an old man-made landscape like the juniper heath. Shepherds and their regularly grazing flocks see to it that the meagre grass is kept short, preventing bushes and shrubs from growing. People who like to hike or go for a walk love it here, and in winter, when there is enough snow, the heath is a popular place for cross-country skiing. In the absence of shepherds and flocks, the heath needs to be mowed and thinned regularly.

Es brodelt im Aachtopf (rechts). Im Durchschnitt quellen hier in Aach bei Engen – nahe dem Bodensee! – an die 9000 Liter Wasser in der Sekunde aus dem verkarsteten Boden, Wasser, das zum überwiegenden Teil aus der jungen Donau kommt, die zwischen Immendingen und Tuttlingen-Möhringen und später bei Fridingen versinkt (versickert). Aus dem reich sprudelnden Aachtopf wird schnell ein ansehnliches Flüßchen, die Aach, die zum Bodensee fließt. In manchen Jahren ist das Donaubett unterhalb von Immendingen wochenlang völlig ausgetrocknet (unten).

The Aachtopf is bubbling over (left). Here at Aach near Engen – close to Lake Constance! – an average of about 9000 liters of water per second gush forth from the karst ground. The water mostly comes from the young Danube, which seeps into the ground between Immendingen and Tuttlingen-Möhringen and later Fridingen. The richly bubbling Aachtopf soon becomes a shapely stream, the Aach, which flows in Lake Constance. In some years, the bed of the Danube below Immendingen dries out for weeks on end (below).

Die Donauversickerung stellt ein Phänomen dar: Der später so mächtige, gut 2800 km lange Strom ist im Sommer und Herbst an seinem Oberlauf oft praktisch verschwunden. Schuld sind die stark durchlässigen Kalkschichten. Das Donauwasser steigt dann nach rund 12 km – von Immendingen – und 18 km Weg – von Fridingen – im Aachtopf wieder an die Oberfläche. Für diesen Lauf durch den Weißen Jura braucht es zwischen einem und vier Tagen. So darf der weit kürzere Rhein die viel längere Donau wenigstens indirekt zu seinen Nebenflüssen zählen.

The seeping away of the Danube is quite a phenomenon: This mighty river, about 2800 km long, in summer and fall often vanishes completely at its upper course. This is due to the effects of extremely permeable layers of limestone. The Danube water once more rises to the surface at the Aachtopf after a distance of 12 km from Immendingen and 18 km from Fridingen. For this stretch through the White Jurassic mountains, the water needs between one and four days. Thus, a by far shorter Rhine may count the much longer Danube among its tributaries, at least indirectly.

as Durchbruchstal der Donau
zwischen Tuttlingen und Sigmaringen gehört zu den schönsten
Naturerscheinungen in Deutschland. Hier als Beweis der Blick von
den Schaufelsen bei Hausen im Tal.
Der Flußdurchbruch im Südwesten
der Alb verdankt seine malerische
Szenerie weniger der Kraft des
Wassers als vielmehr einem geo-
logischen Vorgang seit der Zeit des
Tertiär. Gebirgshebung, Eiszeit,
Schmelzwasser und Verkarstung –
vieles wirkte und wirkt dabei
zusammen. Ständig kommen
Wanderer und Naturfreunde, um
das Tal mit den strahlend hellen
Felswänden und die wildroman-
tischen Aus- und Tiefblicke zu
bewundern.

The valley formed by the river
breaking through the mountain
range between Tuttlingen and
Sigmaringen is one of the most
splendid natural sights in Germany, as illustrated by the view
from the Schaufelsen rocks near
Hausen im Tal. The break-through
in the southwestern part of the
Alb owes its picturesque scenery
less to the power of the water
than to an ongoing geological
process that started in the
Tertiary: Rising mountains, Ice
Ages, melting snow and ice and
the formation of karst – a multitude of factors working together.
The bright, shining walls of rock
and the romantic views down into
the valley and across the land are
admired by a continuous stream
of hikers and nature lovers.

Die Nebelhöhle (rechts): Sie liegt auf oder besser in der Reutlinger Alb nahe Sonnenbühl-Genkingen. Aus mancherlei Gründen wurde sie eine der bekanntesten in Baden-Württemberg. 1486 zum ersten Mal erwähnt, erlangte die Höhle 1803 überregionale Bedeutung durch einen prominenten Besuch: Der Kurfürst von Württemberg, der nachmalige König Friedrich I., geruhte sie zu besichtigen, was sich alsbald im ganzen Lande herumsprach. Die Nebelhöhle mit ihrer Länge von 280 m, ohne Seitengänge, wurde zum Publikumsmagneten. Vollends, als sie dann auch noch von Wilhelm Hauff in seinem Roman „Lichtenstein" als Versteck des flüchtenden Herzogs Ulrich Anfang des 16. Jahrhunderts Erwähnung fand. Alljährlich gibt es seitdem ein Nebelhöhlenfest.

Auf dem Bild der rechten Seite die Große Scheuer auf dem Rosenstein über Heubach, eine 40 m lange Felsgrotte.

The Nebelhöhle cave (left) is situated on, or better in, the Reutlinger Alb mountains near Sonnenbühl-Genkingen. For a number of reasons, it is one of the most famous caves in Baden-Württemberg. Mentioned for the first time in 1486, the cave became known beyond the boundaries of the state when the Elector of Württemberg, who later was to be King Friedrich I, deigned to visit it, a fact that made the rounds in the state. The cave, 280 m long and without side tracts, soon was a popular tourist sight. Wilhelm Hauff's choice of it in his novel "Lichtenstein" as the hiding-place of Duke Ulrich on his flight at the beginning of the 16th century provided added interest. Ever since, there has been an annual Nebelhöhle festival.

On the picture on the right, the Große Scheuer on the Rosenstein above Heubach, a rock cave measuring 40 m in length.

Rechts: *Von links nach rechts die drei Kaiserberge Stuifen, Hohenstaufen und Rechberg. Hier sind wir im Stauferland, der Heimat des berühmten Kaisergeschlechts, deswegen der Name Kaiserberge. Friedrich I. – Barbarossa oder Rotbart – gründete die in unmittelbarer Nähe liegenden Städte Schwäbisch Gmünd und Göppingen. Friedrich II., der seine Heimatsprache schon nicht mehr beherrschte, regierte sein gewaltiges Reich von Sizilien und Apulien aus. Die Herrschaft der Staufer, der Herzöge von Schwaben, endete mit Konradin, der 1268 in Neapel hingerichtet wurde. Die Kaiserberge sind, wie viele andere Erhebungen knapp vor dem Rand der Alb, Zeugenberge. Sie zeugen von der in Urzeiten weiter nach Nordwesten reichenden Albtafel aus Weißjurakalken und von den Veränderungen in Jahrtausenden und -millionen: durch Regen, Sturm, Frost, Erdbeben und Erdrutsche. Auf der rechten Seite winterlich erstarrte Obstbaumhänge am Fuße der Alb im Neidlinger Tal mit der Ruine Reußenstein. Deutlich sind der Albtrauf und die anschließende Hochfläche zu erkennen.*

Left: *From left to right, the three imperial mountains Stuifen, Hohenstaufen and Rechberg. This is Staufer country, the home of the famous imperial dynasty – thus the epithet imperial mountains. Friedrich I Barbarossa – or Redbeard – founded the nearby towns Schwäbisch Gmünd and Göppingen. Friedrich II, who no longer spoke the language of his native country, governed his mighty kingdom from Sicily and Apulia. The rule of the Staufer family, Dukes of Swabia, ended in 1268 with Konradin being executed in Naples in 1268. The imperial mountains, like other elevations close to the edge of the Alb, are so-called "indicators." They indicate that in an earlier age, the Alb shelf, which consists of limestone from the White Jurassic period, extended further to the Northeast, and they also testify to the changes effected by rain, storms, frost, earthquakes and landslides in the course of thousands and millions of years. On the right, a view of wintry hillsides with fruit trees in the Neidling valley in the foothills of the Alb, and of the castle ruin Reußenstein. The steep decline of the "Albtrauf" and the high plain beyond are easily discernible.*

Es braucht nicht viel Phantasie angesichts dieser Weitblicke von der Alb abwärts oder an ihrem Rand entlang, um nachvollziehen zu können, was der Dichter Gustav Schwab beschrieb. Er sah in der Alb ein Gemälde, „wenn die Luft nicht dünstig, der Horizont an den Bergen blau ist und die Abendsonne einen Strahl auf diese Ferne wirft". Dann würde „die Farbe des Gebirgs in ein durchsichtiges Blau verklärt, über das der Sonnenschein eine leichte Röte gießt, in der bald mehr Wechsel der Formen hervortritt, als das Auge früher geahnt".

Considering these views down from the Alb or along its edge, not much imagination is required fo feel with the poet Gustav Schwab that the Alb resembles a painting "if the air is not hazy, the horizon above the mountains blue and the evening sun casts a ray of light into the very distance." He goes on that in such cases "the colour of the mountains appears a transparent blue, steeped in a delicate red by the rays of sunlight and producing a change of forms that the eye could have never anticipated."

Die Klosterkirche von Blaubeuren spiegelt sich im Blautopf. Die Grafen von Tübingen gründeten Ende des 11. Jahrhunderts hier ein Benediktinerkloster. Ein dann entstehender Marktflecken entwickelte sich zur Stadt. Heute führt das Seminar der evangelischen Landeskirche im ehemaligen Kloster bis zum Abitur. Der Blautopf ist insbesondere durch die Poesie des schwäbischen Lyrikers Eduard Mörike zum populärsten Quelltopf der Schwäbischen Alb geworden. Die starke Quelle mit jahreszeitlich bedingten, enormen Schwankungen kann aber auch jeden noch so nüchternen Menschen bezaubern.

Rechte Seite: Die Bürger von Ulm, der ehedem freien Reichsstadt an der Donau, leisteten sich schon im ausgehenden Mittelalter eine gewaltige Kirche, das Münster. Im 19. Jahrhundert reichte es dann zur Vollendung des Turmtorsos, der so mit 161 m zum höchsten Kirchturm der Welt wurde.
Die Anziehungskraft des Münsterplatzes unter dem mächtigen Turm ist noch gewachsen, seit vor ein paar Jahren das Ulmer Stadthaus als moderner Kontrapunkt gesetzt worden ist – nach langen und zeitweise erbitterten Diskussionen.

The monastery church of Blaubeuren reflected in the Blautopf. The Benedictine monastery was founded by the counts of Tübingen at the end of the 11th century. The market site then developed into a town. Today, the former monastery houses the Protestant State Church Seminar a high school. The Blautopf, the most popular headwaters in the Schwäbische Alb, came to fame with the lyrics of the Swabian poet Eduard Mörike. The powerful spring goes through enormous seasonal changes, but charms even the most sober of people.
Right: The citizens of Ulm, a formerly free city on the Danube, already started building their imposing church, a Gothic cathedral in the late Middle Ages. The torso of the tower, with its 161 m highest spire in the world, was finally completed in the 19th century. The charm of the cathedral square below the mighty tower has increased since the Ulmer Stadthaus was built as a modern counterpoint a few years ago, after a period of long and at times embittered in-fighting.

Im Märchen von der „schönen Lau" erzählt Mörike wundersame Dinge und schwärmt von den Verfärbungen, der Kraft und der Klarheit der Karstquelle, die aus dem Sickerwasser der Blaubeurer und Laichinger Alb gespeist wird. Schwaben denken beim Blautopf an den Zungenbrecher „'s leit a Klötzle Blei glei bei Blaubeura", den Mörike in seine Erzählung aufgenommen hat. Bei der schönen Lau, einer Wasserprinzessin, fand ein Hirtenbub das Klötzle Blei, das den Menschen unsichtbar machen konnte.

In the fairy tale of the "beautiful Lau", Mörike recounts wondrous happenings and raves about the colors, the power and the clarity of the karst spring fed by water seeping through the rock of the Blaubeuren and Laichingen Albs. The Blautopf usually makes Swabians think of the tongue-twister "'s leit a Klötzle Blei glei bei Blaubeura", which Mörike integrated into his fairy tale. A shepherd's boy found the "Klötzle Blei" – a lump of lead –, which rendered humans invisible, with "the beautiful Lau", a water princess.

Oberschwaben

„Stuagert, Ulm ond Biberach, Meckabeura, Durlesbach …" Das berühmte Lied von den schwäb'schen Eisenbahnen führt uns geradewegs ins Oberschwäbische, in das Land zwischen dem südlichen Rand der Alb und dem Bodensee. Es führt uns in das „Himmelreich des Barock", wie schwärmerisch-beseelt gesagt wird, oder naturalistischer, in das „Land der tausend Seen, Weiher, Moore und Riede". Auch hier hat uns die Eiszeit diese Landschaft geschenkt, die so schön ist und so eigenartig und die schon etwas nach „Süden" schmeckt, der ja auch über den nahen Alpen beginnt, gleich hinter dem Bodensee. Mit dem Süden ist Oberschwaben durch die Handelswege, an denen sich wichtige, durch Patrizier geprägte Zentren bildeten, lange schon verbunden.

Das beginnt bereits in Ulm, dem „Tor zu Oberschwaben", mit dem 161 m hohen, höchsten Kirchturm der Welt. Von ihm aus läßt sich Oberschwaben bis hin zum See und zu den Alpen überblicken. So recht in Oberschwaben sind wir dann in Biberach, in Saulgau, in Ravensburg oder im württembergischen Allgäu, in Wangen, Kißlegg, Isny oder Leutkirch. Um die Städte breitet sich Bauernland aus, mit Höfen, deren Größe die in anderen Regionen des Landes oft übertrifft. Aus diesem Grunde entstand auch ein anderes Volkslied, das „reich und arm" besingt, das von Schlehen im Oberland erzählt und von Trauben im Unterland. Damit sind die Gegensätze im alten Württemberg gemeint, die soziologischen wie klimatischen. Im Oberland, in Oberschwaben, fanden früher auch „Schwabenkinder" Zuflucht, Kinder, die in ihrer Heimat – in abgelegenen Alpentälern Vorarlbergs oder Tirols – nicht mehr am Leben erhalten werden konnten und deshalb zu den reichen Bauern in Schwaben über dem See geschickt wurden, bei denen sie arbeiten mußten. So war das in vergangenen Zeiten.

Noch heute aber ist der Wohlstand in Oberschwaben zu spüren, verbunden mit einer Ruhe, die aus dem bäuerlichen Leben zu wachsen scheint. Man braucht die ausgetretenen Pfade nur zu verlassen, um Oasen der Stille zu finden, um wahrhaftig „die Seele baumeln zu lassen" und darüber hinaus viel für seine Gesundheit zu tun. Denn Oberschwaben ist reich an heilsamen Wassern und Mooren, die in den Kurbädern und Badeorten seit Generationen therapeutisch genutzt werden.

Upper Swabia

"Stuagert, Ulm ond Biberach, Meckabeura, Durlesbach …" The famous song of the Swabian trains is a good introduction to Upper Swabia, to the region between the southern edge of the Alb mountains and Lake Constance. This is the "heavenly kingdom of the baroque", as romantics like to call it, or, more soberly, "the land of a thousand lakes, ponds, moors and fens." Here, too, the Ice Age has left behind a landscape already reminiscent of „the South" – which, indeed, begins on the other side of the nearby Alps, just south of Lake Constance. Naturally, Upper Swabia has been linked with the South through trade routes, along which important centers developed, for many centuries.

Ulm, the "Gate to Upper Swabia" with its tower of 161 m – the highest church spire in the world – is a good example of a proud patrician lifestyle. The spire affords a view of Upper Swabia, the Lake and the Alps. Further into Upper Swabia, there are Biberach, Saulgau, Ravensburg, and in the Württemberg Allgäu region Wangen, Kißlegg, Isny or Leutkirch. The towns are surrounded by cultivated land belonging to farms that often are larger than in other regions of the state. This gave rise to yet another folk song about "the rich and the poor", about "sloes in the highlands" and "grapes in the lowlands", describing the contrasts in Old Württemberg with respect to both sociology and climate. The highlands, Upper Swabia, also used to be a refuge for so-called "Swabian children", children for whom there was not enough to go around at home – remote valleys in Vorarlberg and Tyrol – and who were sent to rich farmers across the lake as farmhands. That's how it was in the old days.

The wealth of Upper Swabia is noticeable even today, as is a certain calm which seems to spring from rural life. Oases of peace are plentiful if one only leaves the old, well-trodden paths. Here, people may still truly "let their soul take a rest" and, besides, do much for their health: Upper Swabia is rich in medicinal springs and moors which have been put to therapeutic use in spas and health resorts for generations.

Left: The monastery Obermarchtal, here above a foaming Danube, is a good starting point for a tour of the baroque sights of Upper Swabia if one enters the Alb from the north. Obermarchtal, the main seat of the Premonstratensian order, dates back to the year 776. At the end of the 17th century, the order commissioned two master builders of the Vorarlberg School, the brothers Thumb and Franz Beer, to build the monastery church. It was to become a model for the emerging baroque style in Upper Swabia.
Above: At Riedlingen, as is the case in other places close to the Danube or around Federsee lake, storks built their nests in the middle of town on high gables or roofs.

Links: Das Kloster Obermarchtal über der sich schäumend gebenden Donau – ein guter Auftakt für eine oberschwäbische Barockreise, wenn man von Norden her über die Alb kommt. Obermarchtal, das Reichsstift der Prämonstratenser, geht auf das Jahr 776 zurück. Der Orden gab Ende des 17. Jahrhunderts Baumeistern der Vorarlberger Schule, den Gebrüdern Thumb und Franz Beer, den Auftrag für seine Klosterkirche. Sie sollte zu einem Modell für die Entwicklung des Barock in Oberschwaben werden.
Rechts: In Riedlingen nisten, wie in anderen Orten nahe der Donau oder rund um den Federsee, mitten im Kern der Gemeinde Störche auf hohen Giebeln oder Dächern.

Rechts der Bacchussaal im Schloß Tettnang. Die Stadt Tettnang liegt mitten im oberschwäbischen Hopfenanbaugebiet und darf gleich auf drei Schlösser stolz sein. Das repräsentative Neue Schloß vom Anfang des 18. Jahrhunderts mit seinen vier Ecktürmen mußte nach einer Feuersbrunst 1753 wieder aufgebaut werden. Mit der dabei vorgenommenen neuen Innenausstattung kostete das den Grafen von Montfort-Tettnang so viel Geld, daß er sich 1780 gezwungen sah, seine ganze Herrschaft an Österreich zu übertragen. Das tat den herrlichen Stukkaturen des Joseph Anton Feuchtmayer keinen Abbruch. In der Schloßkirche und im Bacchussaal freut sich die Nachwelt heute noch an den Kunstwerken.

Auf dem Bild der rechten Seite das Deckenfresko der Dorfkirche in Steinhausen, „der schönsten in der Welt", wie nicht nur Oberschwaben meinen.

Drei der ersten vier Bilder dieses Kapitels machen eines klar: Oberschwaben ist ein traditionell geformtes, frommes Land, das eigentlich – will man es richtig kennenlernen – erwandert werden sollte. Man kann sich jedoch auch auf die Wegweiser der Oberschwäbischen Barockstraße verlassen, die von Kirche zu Kirche, zu Klöstern, aber auch zu Schlössern, Dörfern und Städten führt, zu Zielen, die ebenso religiös-herrschaftliche Macht ausstrahlen wie bäuerlich verwurzelte Erdverbundenheit und stolzes Patriziertum.

On the left, the „Bacchus Room" at Tettnang Palace. The town of Tettnang is situated in the middle of the hops-growing region of Upper Swabia and may boast of no less than three palaces. The representative New Palace with its four corner towers dating from the beginning of the 18th century had to be rebuilt after a fire in 1753. This and the new interior purchased by the Count of Montfort-Tettnang on this occasion cost so much money that in 1780 the count was forced to make over his entire domain to Austria. This, however, did not diminish Joseph Anton Feuchtmayer's wonderful stucco ornaments. The artefacts can still be admired today in the palace church and the Bacchus Room.

The picture on the right shows the ceiling fresco in the Steinhausen village church, the „most beautiful one in the world" according to – not only – Upper Swabians.

As becomes clear from these pictures, Upper Swabia is a country characterized by tradition and piety, and people who really want to get to know the region should explore it on foot. Another method is to follow the signposts designating the "Route of the Upper Swabian Baroque", which leads from church to church and to monastery, but also to palaces, villages and towns – sights which stand for both ecclesiastical power and local down-to-earth rural traditions as well as proud patrician values.

nks: Über den Dächern von
Blegg, die barocke Turmhaube
er Pfarrkirche St. Gallus. Der
escheiden wirkende Ort im würt-
mbergischen Allgäu wartet
merhin mit zwei Schlössern auf:
em Alten Schloß der fürstlichen
milie Waldburg-Wolfegg-Wald-
e und dem Neuen Schloß der
irsten Waldburg-Zeil-Wurzach.
itten im Städtchen liegt ein für
ese Landschaft typischer See.
f dem Bild rechts ein Blick auf
as Rathaus von Wangen im Allgäu
it dem Pfaffenturm und der
arrkirche. Wangen wurde im
3. Jahrhundert durch den Staufer-
aiser Friedrich II. zur freien
eichsstadt erhoben und war
reuzungspunkt wichtiger Fern-
raßen, auf denen der Handel
uer durch Europa abgewickelt
urde. Reichtum und Ansehen
rlangte die Stadt im Mittelalter
uch durch den Fleiß ihrer Hand-
erker, vor allem ihrer Schmiede.

*Far left: Above the roofs of
Kißlegg, the baroque cap of the
steeple of the parish church
St. Gallus. Despite its two palaces –
the Old Palace of the Waldburg-
Wolfegg-Waldsee dynasty and the
New Palace of the princes of Waldburg-Zeil-Wurzach – the town in
the Württemberg Allgäu region
makes quite a modest impression.
A lake typical for this region occu-
pies the very center of the town.
The picture on the left shows a
view onto the city hall of Wangen
im Allgäu, with the Pfaffenturm
tower and the parish church.
Wangen was made a free city in
the 13th century by the Staufen
emperor Friedrich II. Important
routes crossed here, connecting
trade centers all over Europe. In
the Middle Ages, the town also
acquired wealth and fame
through its industrious craftsmen,
above all its smiths.*

Zur Verehrung der Heiligblut-
reliquie des Klosters Weingarten
findet seit 1529 an jedem Freitag
nach Christi Himmelfahrt eine
Reiterprozession statt (unten).
Darüber sind Chorknaben in Berg
bei Weingarten gerade dabei, am
Palmsonntag mit Buchsbaum und
bemalten Eiern geschmückte
Kreuze in die Kirche zu tragen –
Zeichen einer fortwährenden
tiefen Frömmigkeit.
Rechte Seite: Ein Ausschnitt von
Ravensburg, der Stadt der Türme
und Tore, zeigt den fast 50 m
hohen „Mehlsack" oder Weißen
Turm und das Obertor mit Turm.
Der kleine Erker daran hatte früher
den Zweck, anrückenden Feinden
heiße Köpfe zu bereiten. Hinab-
gegossenes Pech sollte sie das
Fürchten und Flüchten lehren.

The adoration of the Holy Blood
Relic at Weingarten monastery ha
been celebrated every year since
1529 with a mounted procession
on the friday after the Ascension
of Christ church holiday (below).
Above, choir boys of Berg near
Weingarten in the process of
carrying crosses decorated with
boxwood and painted eggs into
the church on Palm Sunday – sign
of an ongoing deep piety.
Right: This view of Ravensburg,
the town of towers and gates,
shows the "Flour Sack", or White
Tower, which is almost 50 m high,
and the Obertor gate with its
tower. Once upon a time, the
small oriel was used for giving
onrushing enemies hot heads as
heated pitch was poured down to
scare them off and put them to
flight.